America in B

A Survival Guide

by

Paul Tarrant

First Edition

Newjoy Press
Ventura California USA

i

To Gail
With much affection
Paul Tarrant

American Travelers in Britain
A Survival Guide

Paul Tarrant

Published by:
Newjoy Press
Post Office Box 3437
Ventura, CA 93006-3437 U.S.A.

All rights reserved. No part of this book may be reproduced or transmitted in any form or by any means, electronic or mechanical, including photocopying, recording or by any information storage and retrieval system without written permission from the author, except for the inclusion of brief quotations in a review.

Copyright © 1997 by Paul Tarrant
Printed in the United States of America

The Library of Congress Data
Tarrant, Paul
American Travelers in Britain: A Survival Guide / by Paul Tarrant. - First Edition
Includes bibliographical references and index
ISBN 1-879899-05-1: $15.95
1. Travelers' Assistance
2. Travel: Britain
3. Relocation to Great Britain

LOC #97-067145

The Table of Contents

About the Author

Paul Tarrant was born in 1957 at Barton-on Sea on the south side of England. He grew up in the neighboring seaside city of Bournemouth. He attended university in the midlands city of Birmingham, then spent a year in Jerusalem as part of his training for the Anglican priesthood. Returning to England in 1981, he continues his studies at Chichester and Sussex. He was then ordained a priest in London's famous St. Paul's Cathedral.

After serving for eight years in two London parishes, he moved to the United States in 1990, where he became the rector of an Episcopal parish in Taunton, Massachusetts.

Although he dabbled with writing over a number of years and had several articles published in various magazines and newspapers, it was his fascination with the differences between the American and British cultures that prompted him to write this book.

He returned to the United Kingdom in 1996 and is now living in Eyemouth, Scotland. His interests include travel and walks along the beach with his golden retriever, Bathsheba.

Dedication

To my parents, Jean and Colin

For all the support they have given
me over the years.

ACKNOWLEDGMENTS

The author thanks the following persons for their support, advice and encouragement in the preparation of this book.

Ted Devlin
who proofread the original manuscript

Jean & Colin Hill
Joy Dawson

This book is dedicated to them all

Disclaimer

This book is designed to provide information regarding the subject matter covered. It is sold with the understanding that the publisher and author are not engaged in rendering professional services.

Every effort has been made to make this book as complete and accurate as possible. However there may be mistakes both typographical and in content. Therefore, this book should be used as a general guide for travel in Britain and not as the ultimate source of information on the subject.

The purpose of this book is to educate and entertain. The author and Newjoy Press will have neither liability nor responsibility to any person or entity with respect to any loss or damage caused or alleged to be caused, directly or indirectly by the information contained in this book.

If you do not wish to be bound by the above, you may return the book to the publisher for a full refund.

Introduction

Thatched cottages nestling snugly round a village pond; a patchwork quilt of fields - more shades of green than you knew existed; narrow country lanes lined with hedgerows; the gentle scent of wild honeysuckle; a gentle hillside golden with daffodils; dense woodlands carpeted with bluebells - these images of the British landscape will linger long after your vacation ends.

Fill your senses with the wildness of the Scottish highlands and the Welsh mountains; 5,000 miles of towering cliffs, sandy coves, windswept marshes and magnificent estuaries.

Look with awe on the human contribution: vast medieval castles, majestic cathedrals and glorious stately homes. They ring with centuries of the history of a great nation.

Enjoy the hustle and bustle of the cities such as cosmopolitan London and the rugged magnificence of Edinburgh, Scotland's capital.

Explore medieval cities with their wealth of historic buildings and sites. York and Winchester are two with special character.

Visit Manchester, Birmingham and Glasgow if industrial and commercial centers are interesting to you,

Visit market towns. Many have been in business for centuries.

Don't leave out quintessential British villages, each with their church and pub.

All these places are found in Britain along with customs and traditions often dating back thousands of years.

Most of all, Britain is her people. Proud island inhabitants trying to come to terms with the changed realities of the twentieth century.

Many Britains long for the gentler, kinder days before WW II when Britain ruled the waves - and often waived the rules.

When I came to America seven years ago to live and work, I learned that in many ways British and American people have different customs and outlooks on life. Keep an open mind when you travel. Don't expect people to be just like you - respect the differences. Don't be afraid to ask questions. This book will help you avoid some of those embarrassing or confusing experiences which might mar an otherwise enjoyable experience.

More Americans and Canadians than ever before are visiting Britain, often for the first time. Many first-timers choose guided tours, then return later to explore at their own pace.

Those who have the curiosity to explore beyond the main tourist attractions will discover some of the world's most beautiful and peaceful countryside, fascinating historical sites and bustling cities.

Get to know the people. You will find a warmth and generosity of spirit quite unlike the stuffy image portrayed in books and on television. Be sensitive to the national differences within Britain. "English" is not synonymous with "British" as any Scot or Welshman will firmly, but politely, point out. To describe Queen Elizabeth as the "Queen of England" will not win you any Scottish or Welsh friends.

The goals of this book are to help you gain insight into what makes Britains tick; to give you information about British customs and language and to help you avoid awkward situations.

Inevitably, it has many generalizations - always dangerous in a land as diverse as Britain. Use the book as a general guide, then, with an open mind, enjoy!

SECTION ONE

PEOPLE AND CUSTOMS

5

Chapter One

A POTTED HISTORY

Britain was part of the continental European land mass until about 6,000 B.C. when it was cut off from the rest of the continent by rising sea levels. Migration into Britain began well before the flooding of the land bridge and continues up to the present.

Among the earliest arrivals were the Celts who arrived 2,500 to 3,000 years ago. Subsequent bands of immigration pushed the Celts to the west and north into what is now Wales, Scotland, Cornwall and Ireland. The language of the Celts survives in Irish Gaelic, Scots Gaelic and Welsh. Another variant, Cornish, all but disappeared centuries ago despite efforts to revive it.

The Romans, led by Julius Caesar, launched two unsuccessful invasions before they arrived on the south coast of what is now England in 43 A.D. They added England to the Roman Empire. The Romans established commercial and political centers and built a network of roads and forts. They built Hadrian's Wall to keep Pict raiders from the north out of Roman Britain. Many remnants of their society are still to be seen in England. The Romans abandoned Britain after 400 years.

When the Roman legions left in 410, waves of

Angles, Saxons and Jutes arrived from Germany. They vied with Danish raiders for control of the country from the eighth to the eleventh centuries. During this time they established regional kingdoms such as Wessex (the land of the West Saxons) and Mercia.

The Anglo-Saxons were capable farmers. They brought an essential pattern of farming and a rotational field system with them. Their system is still in evidence today.

Although Christianity was well established in other parts of Britain, in 597 Pope Gregory dispatched the missionary Augustine to convert the English. Augustine first arrived in Kent where he converted a local king to the Christian faith. He made his base at Canterbury.

The last successful invasion of the island was in 1066. William the Conqueror invaded from Normandy and defeated the Saxons in the Battle of Hastings. He made London his capital, replacing Winchester - the Saxon capital.

One of William's outstanding achievements was the Domesday Book. Listed in it are the landowners; the value of their holdings; the number of villagers and cottagers; the number of animals and so forth.

Tension between the French-speaking Normans and the Saxons was prevalent for centuries. As the cultures merged and the common English language developed, the country became united.

Opposition by nobles to royal abuse of authority forced King John to sign the *Magna Carta* in 1215. It was a guarantee of rights and the rule of law led to the basics of the parliamentary system of government.

During this period, thousands of knights traveled to the Holy Land in a series of Crusades to defend the Christian holy sites against the Ottomans. At the same time, the English overran Wales, uniting the two countries.

English dynastic claims to large sections of France led to the Hundred Years War (1338 - 1453). The war, battled intermittently, eventually led to the loss of French possessions.

The War of the Roses, a long civil war (1455-1485) concluded with the establishment of the Tudor dynasty.

At long last a distinctive English civilization flourished. There was economic prosperity with the long periods of domestic peace.

Henry VIII broke with the Catholic Church over the matter of his divorce from Catherine of Aragon. The matter eventually led to the foundation of the Church of England in 1534.

Under the rule of Elizabeth I, Britain's naval power increased dramatically. Trade with Europe and the Orient expanded rapidly and colonies were established in the New World.

When Elizabeth I died in 1603, the English and Scottish crowns were united. James VI of Scotland became James I of Great Britain. The countries were not officially linked until the Act of Union of 1707. Then the Union Flag (the Union Jack) became the national emblem.

A struggle between Parliament and the Stuart Kings led to the English Civil War (1642-1649) and the execution of Charles I. Britain became a republic under the puritan, Oliver Cromwell.

The monarchy was restored in 1660 and Charles II became king. He was known as the Merry Monarch.

When Charles II died, his brother succeeded him as James II. He was a Roman Catholic.

In 1688 a bloodless, called Glorious, revolution confirmed the sovereignty of Parliament and replaced James II with the Protestant William of Orange. This sovereignty was strengthened in the eighteenth and nineteenth centuries.

Technological and entrepreneurial innovations led to the Industrial Revolution. A mass exodus from rural areas to growing industrial cities occurred.

The thirteen American colonies were lost but they compensated for this - to some degree - by the growth of the Empire in Canada, India and parts of Africa. Britain's role in the defeat of Napoleon in 1815 strengthened its position as the leading world power.

The extension of the voting franchise in 1832 and 1867 was accompanied by the establishment of the union movement to protect the rights of workers. In the mid to late 1800s, the development of universal public education was a drastic social change accompanying the spread of industrialization and urbanization. The population grew rapidly and poverty as described in the novels of Charles Dickens was rife.

During the long reign of Victoria, vast tracts of land in Africa and Asia were added to the Empire.

Just prior to World War I, British power and prestige were higher than they had ever been. Britain experienced massive casualties in the war. Despite being victorious, during the war and the postwar period the nation experienced the beginning of an economic slide.

Ireland became independent in 1921, followed by equally successful bids for independence by other colonies, including India.

Despite eventual victory with the help of the United States, Canada and other allies, World War II brought further economic decline. The war left whole sections of London and other industrial cities in rubble. Through it all, the spirit of the British people remained intact.

After WWII, a new Labor Government established the National Health Service. The social welfare programs brought universal health and social security coverage to all Britons.

Several major industries and institutions were nationalized and industrial growth continued through the 1950s. Britain's economic prospects improved.

The 1960s was a period of tremendous social and political upheaval. One drastic consequence included a miner's strike in 1970. During this strike, a three-day work week was in effect as businesses and shops closed to save power. One result was the resignation of Edward Heath's Conservative Government

Britain became a member of the European Community in 1970. At the same time, many of her colonies were becoming independent.

Further industrial discontent prompted more political instability. Exceptionally high inflation brought the right-wing Conservative administration of Margaret Thatcher to power in 1980. Under Thatcher, the influence of the unions was greatly reduced. Increased emphasis on private enterprise and the entrepreneurial spirit took over.

Frictions in the country over Britain's role in Europe - or rather, Europe's role in Britain - contributed to Thatcher's downfall in 1990. The more moderate John Major led the conservatives to a surprise victory at the polls in 1993.

Britain sent troops to the Gulf War in 1990.

Conservative popularity reached an all-time low in 1994 leading to the resurgence of a moderate

Labour Party, known as New Labour under the leadership of John Smith, and later, Tony Blair. Tony Blair was recently elected Prime Minister by a large majority.

The Channel Tunnel linking Britain and France was finally opened in 1994.

The relationship between Britain and Europe continue to dominate the British political scene. Of particular concern is the fear of monetary union with a loss of sovereignty from Westminster to Brussels.

Constitutional questions relating to the royal family are of great concern to Britons at this time.

Chapter Two

THE PEOPLE

"We English are good at forgiving our enemies; it releases us from the obligation of liking our friends."   P.D. James

Who's a typical Brit? Since *Upstairs, Downstairs,* Americans and Canadians have seen their stereotypical views of the British affirmed by the appearance on television of a variety of period costume dramas. Older British women all walk, talk and look like Joan Hickson's *Miss Marple.* Older British men all walk, talk and look like Alistair Cooke.

While Miss Maple lookalikes can be seen at church garden parties the length and breadth of the country and Alistair Cooke clones play bowls on sunny summer afternoons at south coast seaside resorts, such genteel stereotypes are about as far from the norm as Pat Buchanan is from the White House.

Stereotypes like these are largely the product of Empire, when Britannia, full of self confidence ruled much of the world. Britain was the powerhouse of the world. An abundant supply of coal nourished her industries.

Things turned awry after World War I and World War II. Virtual bankruptcy and a slow

15

deterioration in Britain's manufacturing base, including a number of serious industrial conflicts, prompted a growth in the labor movement.

The gradual disintegration of the Empire beginning with India in 1947, not to mention the rise of America, led to a gradual erosion of national self-esteem. The old girl was tired, very tired. Yet amid the gloom and doom there were some bright spots:

▸ The founding of a National Health Service, whose mission was to provide free health care for all citizens.

▸ Social welfare programs that virtually eradicated the extreme poverty so common during the so called prosperous Victorian era.

▸ Economic booms, such as the one which prompted Prime Minister Harold MacMillan to announce to the British people in 1957 that they "Never had it so good."

Britain was a peaceful, law-abiding nation. In 1944, George Orwell was able to say, "An imaginary foreigner would be struck by the gentleness, by the orderly behavior of the British crowds, and the lack of pushing and quarreling."

Nevertheless, with each boom came the inevitable bust.

Industrial relations suffered badly in the 1970s. Rampant inflation took hold and strikes were

16

abundant. Britain struggled to find a new role in the world as a member of the European Community.

The General Election success of Margaret Thatcher in 1979 helped turn the nation in a new direction. Private enterprise was encouraged. Tough new legislation weakened the power of the unions. Home ownership was promoted. Brits were encouraged to buy shares. The rich became richer, the poor, poorer. Britain scored a decisive victory over Argentina in the Falklands and national pride, for a short time, was restored. Margaret Thatcher was reelected.

By the early 1990s, another recession led many people to question the kind of society Britain was becoming. The murder of little James Bulger by two young boys in 1993 caused an intense period of navel-gazing. Increased crime - sometimes politically and racially motivated, sometimes violence for violence's sake - brought strong calls for action. Finally, the confusion and bewilderment over Britain's role in Europe figured prominently in the national debate.

The first thing to strike many Americans and Canadians is how cosmopolitan and complex British society is today, especially in London and the larger urban areas. In the post war period, large numbers of immigrants from Britains former colonies have settled there. They are adding an exciting new dimension and richness to the British way of life.

Britain is a pot that has been melting for thousands of years, not just this century. The Celt from what is now northern France and the Alpine regions of Europe was the first wave of immigrants to arrive - around 1000 BC.

Subsequent invasions of the island, especially the Roman conquest of 43 BC, pushed the Celtic tribes into the rugged, hilly regions of Wales, Scotland, Ireland and Cornwall. This explains in part the pride and fiercely independent traits found in the inhabitants of these areas today. (The Romans built Hadrian's Wall to keep the marauding Celtic Picts out of England.)

When the Roman Empire collapsed in the fourth century, much of Britain was overrun by Angles, Saxons and Jutes from what is now Germany. (Many place-names in Britain are from this period. Look for 'ton and 'ham.)

Vikings were the next wave of invaders. Their raids were mostly on the east and south coasts. (Viking place names have many y's, k's and s'.)

One of the most famous dates in English history, 1066, is remembered for the defeat of Saxon King Harold by William, Duke of Normandy. Under William's leadership, the Normans endorsed a highly structured, feudal society. Serious ethnic tensions existed between the conquered Saxons and the Normans. However, the lack of any further successful invasion over the next thousand years allowed the cultures to gradually merge and a fusion of identity to occur.

Recent waves of immigration have brought many Jews fleeing the carnage of continental Europe and Irish, Greek and Cypriot refugees. Added to these are Bangladeshis fleeing the poverty of their native land; Sikhs from the Punjabi; Gujeratis and African Asians escaping from Idi Amin's regime in Uganda; Indians and Pakistanis.

Many of these immigrants have become highly successful entrepreneurs. All have brought their own distinctive cultural and religious identity. Today you will find more religiously active Moslems in Britain than practicing members of the Church of England.

Many Afro-Caribbeans arrived in the 1950s and 1960s. The took on menial jobs the indigenous British did not want, such as garbage collectors. The new immigrants were more loyal to the Queen than many of her own family and more devoutly Anglican than the Bishop of Barchester. They were deeply shocked - not by the gloomy weather - but far more seriously, by the social rejection and racial discrimination they found. Even the church they espoused, rejected them. This led to an explosive growth of black churches throughout London and the larger cities.

While ethnic tension may not be as serious as that experienced in some large U.S. cities, it certainly exists. Many people of color frequently sense the system is stacked against them with educational and employment opportunities favoring Caucasians. The existence of neo-Nazi groups, responsible for attacks of people of color has not helped the situation.

Now, a National Committee for Racial Equality exists. It promotes fair play and equal opportunities for all ethnic minorities. Policies actively promoting *positive discrimination* (affirmative action) are in place.

Certain ethnic groups, determined not to lose their cultural heritage and identity, will occasionally go out of their way to ensure that does not happen. Tensions sometimes exist where ethnic culture, particularly religious beliefs, conflict with the law of the land. For example, books were burned following the publication of Salman Rushdie's *Satanic Verses*. Or as when, some years ago, live animals were slaughtered in a religious ceremony in London. This provoked outrage from the majority and prompted many letters to the *Times*.

Strains within families can exist when younger westernized members of a family clash with older members over questions regarding marriage and morality.

However, the influence of television, radio and newspapers means most people, even across cultural and ethnic divides, seem to retain certain general traits and behavioral characteristics, values, customs and style welded together by one common denominator - the English language.

Some notable, national characteristics . . .
- ▸ Politeness - Brits will apologize even when the fault is clearly not theirs.
- ▸ Warmth - but not the huggy type.
- ▸ Love of the countryside, sunshine and gardens.
- ▸ A self-deprecating sense of humor.
- ▸ Coolness and a stiff upper lip when faced with a crisis.
- ▸ Pride in their history.
- ▸ Dissatisfaction with the weather, marriage, the government, the Church and now, horror of horrors, the royal family.
- ▸ A love of animals, especially the underdog. (You'd think it a breed peculiar to Britain.)
- ▸ A degree of formality - not stuffiness. A Brit will expect to be introduced as Mr. Smith, not Fred - at least the first time.
- ▸ Jealousy of others' success, whether individuals or nations.
- ▸ A profound sense of economic gloom and doom; Britons are always complaining about the government - unless its winning a war somewhere.
- ▸ Poor teeth. No worse than most other nations but a poor comparison with Americans.

Brits are envious of the American or Canadian

way of life and have a tendency to take things at home for granted. Britain has one of the highest standards of living in the world. They just hate it that the French have a higher one.

British expatriates living in America desperately miss the BBC, real pubs, the sense of humor, driving on the left, walking to the shops and public transport. It's interesting to observe that of all the immigrants in America, the Brits are generally the last to consider citizenship. Perhaps it's their abiding sense of loyalty.

While Americans swear allegiance to the flag and all it represents, Brits don't swear allegiance at all. Like the constitution, it's unwritten. However, if they could, they'd be swearing allegiance to Her Majesty, the Queen - personally. The Queen is the symbol of the nation. Brits wouldn't care too much if you tried to burn their flag, but they'd be very upset if you tried to set fire to the Queen - just as they did in 1605 when a certain Guy Fawkes plotted to blow up King James I.

Don't ever refer to Queen Elizabeth as Queen of England. She is, of course, but she's queen of many other places also, including Scotland, Wales and Northern Ireland.

The Queen is constitutional head of a nation which is an amalgamation of these four, once separate countries. The Union Flag (often called the Union Jack) incorporates the red cross on a white background of the flag of St. George (England), the white diagonal cross on the blue background of St. Andrew (Scotland) and the red diagonal cross on a white background of St. Patrick (Ireland). (The patron saint of Wales is St. David.)

Expect Brits to be pleasant and helpful to you. They are proud of their heritage and very keen to show you they have something special to share. Most people gladly help you find your way if you are lost. If the person you ask is not in a great hurry, they will go out of their way (literally) to get you where you are going.

Brits will resent your supposed financial superiority (don't flaunt it too much), they'll hate those bright red pants Chuck is wearing but they will treat you with great respect and warmth - especially away from London.

Even in London, when you are away from the main tourist areas, they will deal you with like a lord. (If you really want to *feel* like a lord, you can buy your own title).

Try to blend in. Some weird and wonderful things will baffle you completely. Keep a stiff upper lip.

Introduce yourself to the locals in a pub but do it gently. Don't announce, "Hi, I'm Brad from Dallas and I really want to know all about you." You'll watch them run a mile!

Break the ice by talking about the weather or ask questions about cricket, or how Manchester United are doing, or "Isn't that something about Michael Barrymore coming out?" Even if you haven't a clue who Michael Barrymore is, you'll be immediately regarded as a chum.

If the person is not interested in talking to you, you'll get a polite but curt, monosyllabic answer.

For heaven's sake, however friendly you are getting, don't give a Brit a hug unless they are drunk. Brits hate to be touched - even in bed.

You will be pleasantly surprised how *warm* British people are once they overcome their initial shyness and you get to know them at a deeper level. Remember, you're likely to have to make the first move.

The Scots

Scots are fiercely proud of their heritage - and justly so. Many regard themselves as the true Brits who predate the Anglo-Saxon invaders - sometimes called Sassenachs - by centuries.

Until the Act of Union in 1707, Scotland and England were separate countries. Edinburgh served as the capital city of Scotland. Even today, Scotland retains its own banknotes; (legal tender in England, also) its own educational and legal systems; its own distinct traditions, customs and culture. Scotland even has its own church called the Kirk - the Church of

Scotland. It is not related to the Established Church of England south of the border.

Scottish national pride came to the fore in the 1970s when vast deposits of oil and natural gas were discovered off the northeast Scottish coast. Scots regard these findings as theirs, not England's. Many Scots would like to have more control over Scottish affairs although a majority would not wish to see a breakup of the United Kingdom.

The English often make fun of the Scots - and the Scots of them. Countless stand-up comedians depict them as stingy and poker-faced serious. In truth, it can be said the Scots are thrifty people - Presbyterianism has seen to that - but mean? No, the Scots are among the most generous people in the world. Certainly they are serious at times but watch out for their acerbic sense of humor - frequently leveled at the English.

Ask a Scot. The best thing to come out of England is the A1, the main highway leading to Scotland.

Wales

Ever since Wales was conquered by England's King Edward I, it has been treated as an appendage of England. However, it wasn't until the Act of Union of 1536 that the English legal and administrative systems were adopted in Wales. Besides the legal system, Wales also shares England's educational and financial systems.

As descendants of the Celtic tribes that fled the Anglo-Saxon invasions, the Welsh share many characteristics of the people of Scotland, including a variation of the Gaelic language. Welsh is spoken by an increasing number of inhabitants as part of a deliberate policy by the Westminster government to appease Welsh nationalist sentiment.

Welsh nationalism was largely confined to northern Wales and Anglesey until hoards of English people began to purchase second homes in the principality. They drove out local persons and deprived others of jobs and livelihoods. Many cottages owned by English were burned down in protest.

These days, things are much quieter. Some television and radio channels broadcast solely in Welsh. A strong movement to preserve Welsh national identity, culture and language are present and the principality is buzzing with the prospect of devolution.

Until recently, the main industries in Wales were coal mining and steel production. Both of them are now a shadow of their former selves but the stresses and strains of industrial life produced a unique spirit of comradeship and solidarity that exists to this day, especially in the valleys of south Wales.

This comradeship, combined with the extraordinary vocal talent seen in the Welsh valleys, helped cultivate some fine male choirs. They are known throughout the world.

Wales has produced fine actors, poets, and singers. Visitors to Wales will find opportunities to hear the fine choirs in the villages and towns.

The hilly terrain of Wales has produced a hardy, resilient and warmhearted people noted for their fiery temper and passionate feelings. Perhaps that is why people of Welsh stock figure so prominently in British political life. They are noted for their gift of oratory.

The Church of Wales, affiliated with the Church of England used to be the established church in Wales but since most of the people are Nonconformists, the church was disestablished early in this century.

Cardiff is the largest city and the capital of Wales.

Conclusion

Britain's self-esteem may have taken a tumble since the British Empire started crumbling. The United States may have usurped her place at the center of world affairs but she still ranks in the top twenty prosperous nations in the world. Life is generally safe, literacy is high and Queen Elizabeth - God bless 'er - is still on the throne.

The sheer durability and grit of the British people, along with their wonderful sense of humor, will see them through. Britain is a nation still trying to find its role in a changed world. The best may be yet to come.

Chapter Three

THE LANGUAGE

"After all, when you come down to it, how many people speak the same language, even when they speak the same language?"

Russell Hoban

British actress, Diana Rigg appears at the beginning and end of every episode of the PBS *Mystery* program. It is her task to decipher and explain what the characters have been talking about to an American audience. Baffled and bewildered by the vocabulary, the idioms and the accents, by references to Marmite, Daddies' sauce and Max Bygraves, they need an interpreter. The British way of life, for that matter, may be the mystery.

It is no coincidence either that many of the episodes of British TV's *Thomas the Tank Engine* are dubbed because Americans could not understand the heavy Liverpudlian accent of Ringo Starr, the original narrator.

An American or Canadian expects language and communication difficulties on a visit to Norway, Nicaragua or Nepal, but Britain? Sure, they have a quaint way of spelling colour with a *u* and pronouncing *z* as zed. An elevator is a *lift* and gas is *petrol* - easy.

Don't kid yourself. Britain's Reuter news agency and the U.S. Associated press list at least twelve pages of common words and expressions requiring translation from American English to British English. You are not going to be free of difficulties. George Bernard Shaw said we are, "Two nations divided by a common language." While this saying has become a cliché, in essence it is true.

In fact, in Britain you can take it a step further and say, "*One* nation divided by a common language." So many and varied are the accents and dialects, you'll believe the Hindu proverb, "Language changes every eighteen or twenty miles."

The two main factors leading to the development of so many accents and dialects is the ethnicity of the population and the geography of the country.

Forms of the language of the earliest settlers, the Celts, still exist in Wales, Scotland, Ireland and Cornwall. The Germanic invaders brought their own language with them. It was the precursor of Old English from which modern English is derived.

The majority of these people could not read or write. They had to rely on speech and memory so over the centuries a highly developed oral tradition developed. It has a strong emphasis on understatement, riddles and poetry and a love of ambiguity, innuendo and word play. These features are still a distinctive part of British English language. England's conversion to Christianity was a slow process. It began with Augustine in 597 AD. The Christians gradually built churches and monasteries. They brought with them the Latin language, enriching the vocabulary of English.

The language received a major boost with the reign of Alfred, King of Wessex in 871. Wessex was threatened at the time by the plundering raids of the Vikings. They had control of much of the rest of England already.

Alfred realized without victory over the Danes, the English language would be replaced with Norse. He successfully raised an army, defeating the Danes at the battle of Ethandune and forcing them to withdraw to the north.

The country was divided. Alfred and the English speaking Saxons in the south, Danes in the north. Alfred realized could not maintain his kingdom without help from outside its boundaries. Somehow he had to gain political control of a country not his. He succeeded by appealing to a shared sense of Englishness and created a sense of national identity for the first time. He encouraged the use of English rather than Latin in education.

The Danes and Saxons lived beside each other for many years. Gradually, the two languages fused into one English language.

The Norman Invasion of 1066 brought drastic

change. French speaking Normans built castles, schools and churches while speaking French, not English. In fact, several Norman monarchs spoke no English. Meanwhile, the common folk continued to speak it.

Over a long period, as the two cultures began to merge, the English language attained the upper hand albeit with a strong French influence. By the time of the Hundred Years War (1337-1454) against France, speaking English gained momentum it never lost again.

In Britain, strong regional accents prevail. Distinguishing them is almost impossible for Brits - as well as visitors.

There have been squabbles over the ownership of the English language ever since the first English settlers became established in America. The early English settlers had to make up words for items they had never encountered before. They borrowed words from the native Americans. The word *squash*, for example, came into the language this way. Other words and expressions we now take for granted originated with early American pioneers.

At one time, controversy took place about which native language would be adopted in America. By 1800, the majority of Americans were of British stock and it was clear English would be *the* language in an improved version.

One of the greatest linguistic separatists in America was Noah Webster. During the 1780s he published three books on English: a speller, a grammar and a reader. The reader was titled *A Grammatical Institute of the English Language.* It sold 80 million copies. Considering the population at the time, this was phenomenal.

The American Speller was widely used in schools. Children were taught to spell *center* instead of *centre; theater* instead of *theatre; tire* instead of *tyre.* Webster's influence on American spelling was enormous. Because of his work, he helped establish a degree of uniformity in American pronunciation.

American English came to the fore after 1945. The U.S. began to dominate the world economy and became the most powerful nation on earth - a position Britain had held not long before. Thus, a different version of English became the dominant international language.

Some practical examples

You've seen minor differences in spelling in words such as *colour* and *humour* with an added u: *centre* and *theatre* with re; *defence* with a c not an s - the list goes on.

Far more important, however, is the fact that in Britain when you stick your left foot in and your left foot out and shake it all about, you're doing the *hokey cokey,* not the *hokey pokey.*

In Britain, when someone asks "How are you?" and you respond, "Good," they will think you are talking about your moral character rather than your state of health. Brits answer the question with "Fine, alright, or well."

Then there are the differences in vocabulary. Quite apart from words I never knew existed before I came to the States, a host of other words and phrases have changed meaning because of time, usage and 3,000 miles of salt water.

As you pick up your *hired* (rented) car, you'll be told how to open the *boot* (trunk) and the *bonnet* (hood).

Other familiar differences include *biscuit* (cookie), *chips* (french fries), *crisps* (potato chips) but did you know the British for diaper is *nappy*? And when baby is crying, you'll stick a *dummy* (pacifier) into his mouth? When you're cold, you'll find *goose pimples* not goose bumps, on your arms and legs. Throw your rubbish into a *dustbin* to be collected by a *dustman*. When you are on the *motorway* (freeway), don't cross the *central reservation* (median).

Smart in Britain refers to being well-dressed rather than intelligent. If you are *mad* in Britain, you are clinically so, not just angry. A *mean* person is a stingy person. *Pants* always refers to underpants. It is a great compliment when you describe someone's living room as *homely*.

If you stop on the *hard shoulder* (emergency

lane) and get hit by a *lorry* (truck), you may have to go to *casualty* (emergency room) in hospital (not in *the* hospital). You could end up in the *operating theatre.*

Ask your British hosts where the *loo* (toilet) is if you want to impress them. They'll fall about laughing if you ask them where the bathroom is. "Why? Do you want to take a bath?" they will chuckle.

The use of prepositions varies, too. North Americans refer to being *on* the team, while Brits talk about being *in* the team. Brits always write *to* somebody instead of just writing somebody. They protest *against* something instead of simply protesting something.

Then there is every comedian's favorites. When your landlady "knocks you up" at 6:00 a.m. it's quite innocent (probably). To *knock someone up* in Britain means to wake them up. If she immediately goes on to offer you a *rubber*, that's innocent, too. (Except it's a strange time to be offering you an eraser.)

If you are male, you may not want to say you are wearing *suspenders.* In Britain, suspenders refers to the devices some women attach to the top of their stockings to hold them up. Men wear *braces* to hold their *trousers* up - as well as to straighten their teeth.

Do you have a skeleton in your *cupboard* (closet) or a *ladder* (run) in your stockings?

Other terms owe their origins to sports. Cricketing terms like *sticky wicket* are use frequently in Britain. *Bowling a maiden over* has nothing to do with sweeping a girl off her feet. Baseball expressions like *touch base* are, thanks to Hollywood, slowly creeping into English usage. An American TV commercial for washing machines using the pun *making a home run* has no deeper meaning to most Brits unless they have lived in the U.S.

Words can be pronounced or inflected quite differently. "I say potato and you say potāto" is a well-known song, but why do Americans and Canadians say *thur-ō* and Brits say *thur-ugh* for the word thorough? Clergy talk about the prophet *I-zay-ah* in the U.S., not *IZE-EYE-AH* as in Britain.

In many words and phrases, the stress is placed on the second syllable in the United States and on the first syllable in Britain. My own name is nearly alway pronounced TarrANT in the States instead of TARRant. And why ROBIN Hood and not Robin HOOD?

Four-syllable words are pronounced by Americans with all four syllables - sec-re-tar-y and cem-e-tar-y are two. In Britain, its sec-re-try and cem-e-try. Brits call a mall, a *mal*. On top of this, you will have a battle with regional accents. Some of them are so strong that even people from other parts of Britain may have to struggle to understand them.

Brand names of some products have become

part of the everyday vocabulary. *Hoover* is commonly used to describe an upright vacuum cleaner even if that company does not manufacture it. To *hoover* means to vacuum clean.

English has come a long way. In Shakespeare's time it was spoken by no more than five or six million. Like all living languages, it continues to evolve. New discoveries and technologies have added new words and expressions to the language as it is spoken on both sides of the Pond. The dramatic advances in global communications ensure English will continue to develop, adapt and expand.

One thing is certain. You will have a lot of fun with the English language when you're in Britain. Maybe you'll begin to see and think of it in ways you never have before.

Chapter Four

THE CLASS SYSTEM

"It is impossible for an Englishman to open his mouth without making another Englishman despise him."

George Bernard Shaw

Viewers of the British PBS series *Keeping Up Appearances* are only too familiar with the ridiculous antics of Hyacinth Bucket (pronounced bouquet) and the inherent snobbery that motivates her and the other characters. They portray an ongoing, conscious attempt to project the correct image. Keeping up with the Joneses and one upmanship are not traits peculiar to the British, but they do seem to have raised them to an art form.

In the United States if money talks, in Britain breeding positively screams. Even when money does talk in Britain (as it increasingly does), it is more likely to influence people if it's old money. Successful, millionaire, used car salespersons simply do not have the same *caché* as failed baronets.

At the top of the national class pyramid is the Royal Family. Britons are shocked when the present generation of royals seem to experience many of the same problems besetting the ordinary folk because royalty is meant to be above it all. They conveniently forget the antics of Charles II or even Edward VII.

Brits expect their Royal Family to be aloof and even mystical - different from the rest - yet complain when Prince William is sent to the Eton School. In a country where the political emphasis has shifted from the private to the public domain and all people are encouraged to become shareholders, citizens increasingly regard the Royal Family as a commodity in which they have a stake.

All native born Americans can aspire to be President. In Britain, no one can aspire to be Britain's Head of State because they have not been born into the family.

Next in rank after the monarchy and the extended royal family come other aristocrats; earls, dukes and baronets. Most of them are descendants of families who supported the monarchy at some perilous stage in its history or who purchased their titles centuries ago from the Crown or government.

Next in line are the professional and senior managerial classes. This class includes lawyers, Civil Service executives, media barons, City entrepreneurs and aging rock stars. Their sole purpose is life, it seems, is not so much the attainment of financial superiority as to be offered a knighthood or some other prestigious honor (CBE, MBE, etc.) by the Queen.

Members of this class are likely to send their children to public schools. There they, in turn, will be molded for knighthood. The ultimate evidence of superiority is to send a son to Eton, Harrow or Winchester Schools. From thence, they go on to Oxford or Cambridge Universities (only these will do). The upper middle class accent, with no trace of regional, is the one that will get you the job and improve your chances of promotion over others.

The middle classes come next. Their goal is to have 2.4 children and own a pleasant semi-detached house with a garage on a tree-lined avenue in north London. In this category are middle-management, owners of shops and *small* businesses (with no desire to become *big* business), teachers and social workers.

They are intensely jealous of anyone with more money and more power. They don't have the desire or inclination to work any harder - so long as they can afford a week in Tenerife and a satellite dish. Their children attend local state or possibly independent schools and are expected to win a place to university (subsidized - though they'd never admit it.)

So-called lower middle classes follow. They were formerly called the working class. This group includes factory workers, shop assistants, mechanics and so on. More or less content with their lot - "except it would be delightful if we had a semi-detached house with a garage and a real brass door knocker in a tree-lined street in the suburbs." Most live in small flats, terraced houses and council houses (the ultimate put-down in Britain.)

Children are sent to the local state school. They are encouraged to aspire to the next rung up the ladder - to become a bank clerk or a Woolworth store supervisor. Academic achievement by the children, particularly winning a place at university, is graspable, but it's all rather *embarrassing*.

Britain has an increasing number of homeless people, both individuals and families. Some survive by living in bed and breakfast or hostel accommodations at the Government's expense. Others live on the street - a particularly harrowing sight in and around the Embankment and Strand areas of London and other urban centers. Soup kitchens, though not as common in Britain as in the U.S., may be found in some inner city areas where a high density of homeless people exist.

The Labour Party was born out of a concern for the working classes. Their goals were to raise the standard of living and to protect and extend workers' rights. They succeeded in most of their goals long ago. Through their efforts everyone has equal health coverage, education and social security.

However, the basic Establishment went unchallenged (Many Labour MPs came from privileged backgrounds.) The entrepreneurial spirit and incentive instilled in Americans from the start has no equivalent in Britain. It seems, in a funny kind of way, the working classes in Britain are content with the status quo. They appear to think it right and proper to be lorded over by the blue-blooded toffs - or anyone who owns a house with a brass door knocker. In fact, the last Labour government ended in some disarray. In the well-remembered *winter of discontent* many of Britain's public and private sector services came to a grinding halt. Ironically, those who had benefitted most from Labour's policies deserted the party in droves at the next General Election.

Perhaps the greatest challenge to the British Establishment has not come from the Labour Party but from the Conservatives. Margaret Thatcher, daughter of a grocer from Grantham in Lincolnshire proved it is all right for the middle classes to have aspirations (Brits are not quite so sure about the working classes.)

Note: Many of the original Pilgrims originated from the same area as Margaret Thatcher.

During fifteen years of Conservative government, the private sector had become increasingly visible. A vastly increased number of people own their homes and shares in newly privatized industries such as British Telecom.

Former Prime Minister John Major is the son of a trapeze artist from south London and the Archbishop of Canterbury, George Carey, is the son of a hospital porter from east London. They typify the spirit of entrepreneurism.

They were educated at Oxford or Cambridge - as are the vast majority of MPs, high-ranking civil servants, bishops and politicians. It is still the Oxbridge rubber stamp that gives respectability to their position and makes it all right for them to become leading figures in the Establishment.

The fair-minded Brits see other flaws in the system. Unemployment has reached a new high. The rich are richer and the poor keep getting poorer.

Despite Government claims to the contrary, many feel the National Health Service is "not what it was." There is talk of reorganizing the Welfare State. Surveys show people would prefer no tax decreases if they would mean a decline in health or education services.

The Establishment is still very much in control but not quite as much in control as it was, say, a quarter century ago. Shopping in Harrod's; attending Eton or Harrow, Oxford or Cambridge; being invited to the Queen's garden parties; owning a few hundred inherited acres; living off unearned income; taking holidays in Mustique and owning a cottage in the country are still unmistakable statements of prestige but not necessarily of power.

Even before the National Lottery, many Britons became instant millionaires by *doing the pools* - betting on the outcome of weekly soccer matches. All their money does not guarantee social acceptance and respect. Accent, education and social background continue to be the major criteria by which people are measured for important work.

In a country that has largely managed to avoid social revolution, *Glorious*- meaning non-violent - revolutions take place and the people prefer things the way they've always been. The social scene has not changed much since the days of Eliza Doolittle, but it has changed - a bit.

"Game plans" and "setting goals" are things the British don't do readily. The game plan is set out and they know their place in it. Well - sort of.

Chapter Five

HEALTH

"Look to your health: and if you have it, praise God. And value it next to a good conscience; for health is the second blessing that we mortals are capable of; a blessing that money cannot buy."
Izaak Walton

Sensible travelers take proper precautions for their trip overseas. Persons with preexisting medical conditions should check with their doctor before leaving home. If you are on medication, check that you have enough to last you the duration of the trip. You must carry *all* medication in clearly marked, original containers.

As far as general health matters go, Britain is one of the world's safest countries to visit. They require no vaccinations or immunizations for entrance into the country. Health and hygiene laws are strictly enforced. You are highly unlikely to contract cholera or malaria. Few animals, insects or other natural phenomena can inflict lasting damage to you. However, there are some dangers.

Depending on which part of North America you are traveling from and even if you sleep on the plane, jet lag can make you feel quite *knackered* (British slang for very tired). The second day will be

47

the worst. As time goes on, the jet lag will gradually diminish. Experts seem to disagree on how best to reduce the effect. In my experience, sleeping on the plane helps significantly.

It is also quite likely you will experience some stomach discomfort after a day or two. This is quite natural when traveling from one country to another. Most foreigners experience the same when visiting the U.S. All water systems have microbes. You may just be experiencing a different set from what you are used to. In case you are really worried, bottled water can be found in most supermarkets. It is not as widely available as in the U.S., however.

If you are staying in a rental accommodation and are worried about drinking the tap water, you can boil it before drinking.

Milk and dairy products are fully pasteurized throughout the country. Look for the *expiry* (expiration) date on carton, bottle or packet. Fresh fruit and vegetables are safe, just follow normal precautions.

See a doctor if you develop symptoms of intestinal upset persisting more than a day or two,.

Over the counter medications are available at *chemists* (pharmacies). You will find much the same range of products as you do in North America, though sometimes under different brand names. More powerful medications are dispensed with a doctor's prescription.

If a *chemist* (pharmacy) is closed, look at the shop window. Posted on it is often a sign listing other local chemists that are open.

At the seashore follow the same precautions you would back home. Watch out for rough water, strong currents and riptides. At most British resorts a red flag flying along the *promenade* (boardwalk) means you should not swim. Stay away from rocks and the *groynes* (breakers) punctuating the shorelines of many coastal towns.

When swimming in rivers and ponds, look out for currents and weeds. Be aware of the pike if you happen to be swimming in a river,

Few dangerous sea animals live in British waters. Sharks are sometimes seen but they are usually basking sharks or another gentle variety of no danger to humans. Portuguese men o'war sometimes drift close to shore, especially along the south and southwestern coasts.

The countryside is generally safe. You may see snakes but only one is a danger. The adder, identifiable by the zig-zag pattern down its back, is poisonous. Adders thrive in heath land areas. They are not aggressive and are usually more afraid of you than you are of them. Call 999 from any public or private phone immediately should you be bitten.

Mosquitoes are not generally a problem but midges and gnats - despite their tiny size - can give a hefty nip. Lotions and sprays to keep them away are widely available. An alternative is to avoid damp, still areas in the summer.

Smoking is discouraged in Britain. They prohibit it in an increasing number of public places, including many restaurants. On public transport and other public places, specific areas may be designated for smokers.

The British are very proud of their National Health Service (NHS) but take great delight in ridiculing it. The NHS was founded in 1947 by the then Labour Government of Clement Attlee. The principle of the service was to offer comprehensive, *free* medical care to all residents, regardless of income.

Naturally, it is not free. The brunt of the cost is borne through taxes and national insurance payments - corresponding roughly to U.S. social security taxes.

Throughout its young life, the NHS has always been something of a political football. The game reached fever pitch during the government of Margaret Thatcher with her government's increasing emphasis on private health insurance and health care.

The Opposition accused the Conservative Government of trying to destroy the NHS. The government claimed it had no such agenda. Political debate on the health service has cooled down but every now and again it comes to the forefront of political debate.

The British public, on one hand, is bitterly

critical of the Service but leaps passionately to its defense when they perceive it to be under fire. Especially so when they are reminded of the massive medical bills incurred in other countries.

Despite its shortcomings, the British National Health Service is one of the finest in the world. Britain, through the work of some of its university teaching hospitals, frequently leads the world in pioneering new treatments and drugs. In recent years, the emphasis has been on health education. They have targeted specific areas such as coronary heart disease, cancer, accidents, mental illness and HIV/AIDS.

Members of the public are encouraged to have regular check ups, though in practice people rarely visit their doctor except for treatment. Free family planning is available. Free breast and cervical cancer screening programs are in operation.

The NHS is essentially a national HMO. Unless Brits experience an acute medical emergency, the General Practitioner (GP) manages health care.

Note: When there is an emergency, a person can dial 999 anywhere in the country, whereupon they are whisked off to hospital.

Surgery required in a life-threatening situation is normally performed immediately. If a person needs non-life threatening surgery, they may have to wait months - even years - for a routine operation in an *operating theatre* (operating room).

Citizens of Canada and the United States are charged for all medical services except those administered by the *casualty department* (emergency room) of an NHS hospital. If you happen to be a U.S. or Canadian citizen run over by a steamroller, you will not be charged if the injuries only require stitching or setting in the casualty department. You will be required to pay if your injuries dictate you must be admitted to a hospital ward.

Your hotel or the local tourism office will be able to supply you with a list of G.P.s in the area. Many of them work in community health centers as part of a team of doctors, nurses, *health visitors* (visiting nurses) and other staff. Unless you have an urgent problem, a doctor will usually be able to see you in a day or two.

A small payment (by American standards) will be charged for the consultation. If the doctor writes you a prescription, be sure you have identification when you go to the chemist to have it filled.

Check your health insurance policy before you leave North America. Some policies cover medical care and other problems when you are overseas but some don't. Canadians are usually covered by their provincial health plans. Students may find their health insurance includes vacations.

If you find you are not covered, there are a huge variety of travel health plans available. Check what each one offers before making a decision.

Chapter Six

SEX AND FAMILY LIFE

"No Sex Please, We're British"
Title of West End play

Although attitudes toward sex are more liberal today than they have ever been, the Puritan streak in Britain means sex is rather embarrassing - a necessary evil we'd rather do without, but can't, or there wouldn't be any little Brits.

Any serious mention of sex produces a nervous titter in many Britons and memories of an illicit encounter behind the bicycle shed when they were fourteen. Therefore, discussion of sex is relegated to humor.

Sexual innuendo of the Benny Hill variety is high on the list of favorite humorous categories. Saucy seaside postcards are a national institution. The butt of humor is, more often than not, the British woman. How they have been able to survive without a serious bra-burning revolution is beyond me.

The British are reserved even when out on the prowl. Developing a successful strategy for marketing oneself is not part of the British way of doing things. Gleaming white Hollywood-film-star teeth, hair transplants and liposuction are rare. Even boys who regard themselves as God's gift to the opposite sex may spend hours plucking up the courage to talk to a young woman on the other side of the dance floor. He may perform elaborate rituals involving posture and eye movements before eventually making verbal contact.

In America, after just an hour's acquaintance you hear all about the person's recent bout with gallstones, sessions with a psychotherapist and the name of the family cat. In contrast, Brits engage in limited conversation with people they have just met. They may talk about the weather and ask, "You come here often?"

Britons flirt, just not *verbally*. They regard "verbal diarrhea" as an illness every bit as serious as gallstones.

Young people meet at parties, pubs, dance clubs and blind dates. The television program *Blind Date* is one of the most popular programs watched. People are meeting more and more frequently through the *Lonely Hearts* classified columns of newspapers and magazines. *Phone sex* telephone lines were stamped out by the government some years ago.

Contraceptives are widely available in Britain. Abortions are performed routinely on the National Health Service.

Britons may not like doing it, but they love reading about sex, especially the "sexploits" of film stars and royals.

Marriage and the Family

The number of marriages in Britain slumped to its lowest level in fifty years - just under 300,000 in 1993. This was a drop of four percent from the previous year. It was the first time since 1943 (when the numbers were affected by war) that the marriage rate dropped below 300,000.

More than a third of the marriages in 1993 were remarriages of one or both parties. At the same time the divorce rate soared to a record 165,000. This means for every two weddings in England and Wales, roughly one marriage ends in divorce.

Fifty-eight percent of the total population over age 16 is married, 27% are single, 9% widowed and 6% divorced. The average age for a first marriage is age 28 for men and age 24 for women. The ages for a first marriage are going up.

When people divorce, the average ages are age 38 for men and 34 for women.

The established Church of England's policy is to not remarry divorced persons in church, though a blessing may be given to a newly married couple.

If Prince Charles wishes to remarry, he may have to do so in the Church of Scotland which does remarry divorced people. However, a remarriage could cause constitutional complications. Among others - the sovereign automatically becomes

Supreme Governor of the Church of England and Defender of the Faith.

A substantial increase in cohabitation has occurred in Britain over the past few years. Many of the persons living together have stable, though non-married, relationships. One half of all births outside marriage are registered by both parents giving the same address as the usual place of residence.

The number of unmarried, pregnant women was 44% of pregnancies - up from 30% just ten years ago. Thirty-four percent of the pregnancies in unmarried women ended in abortion. (Eight percent of married, pregnant women choose abortion).

The average size of the British household has decreased from an average of over four persons to 2.46 in 1990. There are a number of reasons for this dramatic shift. A greater number of people are living on their own. One-parent families and many elderly persons live alone. Housing conditions have improved.

Some politicians and religious leaders attribute many of British society's problems to the breakdown of family life. Family values are a large part of the British agenda, just as in America and Canada.

The British government, worried about current trends, has ordered its civil servants to examine a range of practical steps to be taken to prevent marriage breakdown and give support to couples trying to keep their marriages intact.

A Parliamentary Bill has been introduced to put an end to quickie divorces on grounds of unreasonable behavior or adultery. If it becomes law, it will impose a year-long cooling off period on divorcing couples. The idea is to encourage them to resolve disputes over children and finances before divorces are granted. The big emphasis will be on reconciliation.

Despite the many changes, the total population of Britain has remained stable over the past decade. The proportion of children aged 16 and younger, dropped during the early 1980s. The birth rate is rising again, as baby boomers children have babies themselves.

The increase in the elderly population worries politicians. The National Health Service struggles to cope with increased demands on its resources. By 1990, more than 18% of the population was over the normal retirement age of 65 for men and 60 for women. Compare that with 15% in the early 1960s.

Citizens over retirement age are known by the unflattering title of Old Age Pensioners (OAPs). They qualify for a variety of benefits including free or reduced-cost travel on public transport, free prescriptions and discounts on a variety of merchandise and services. They receive an old age pension if they have been contributing to the National Insurance scheme.

The Government has been encouraging families

to look after elderly parents in the home. However, fiercely independent Brits tend to prefer living alone.

Nursing homes are an option. The costs depend on each individuals financial circumstances. In Britain, nursing homes are generally smaller and more intimate than their North American counterparts.

Chapter Seven

THE SENSE OF HUMOR

"Humor is practically the only thing the English are serious about."
Malcolm Muggeridge

About 200 people attended the Church Supper. After the meal and a short interlude, the entertainment began. A series of irreverent skits based on parish life interspersed with well-known tunes from the musical *Oklahoma* sung to spoof lyrics was presented.

I thought the people would love it - they always did back home. I based the dialogue for the skits on some BBC radio comedy tapes from the 60s and 70s. They had me riotously laughing and helped offset occasional bouts of homesickness.

In one skit, a theatrical impresario visits a booking agency to find some original acts for his show.

"Good morning. I'm looking for some acts for our church show on November 19th. What do you have available?"

"Well, how about starting with a strip tease? I have just the person."

"I'm not sure that would go down well at a church function, but do go on."

"Her name is Deidre. And she does a strip

tease with a difference."

"*Yes . . .*"

"*Normally she's the bearded lady at the circus. Has hair down to her ankles.*"

"*So what does she do?*"

"*Comes on and shaves. Very special. Very different. Only does it every two years - takes her two years to grow it back again.*"

I had roared with laughter when I first heard the skit on a retired episode of the classic BBC 60s radio program, *Round the Horn* - which still has a cult following in Britain. Yet no one in this American audience, save a few expatriate Brits in a distant corner, even smiled.

Afterwards I asked one of the audience why the skit was such a flop. "We just didn't think it was funny," she said. So there.

Later on, reflecting on that experience reminded me that British humor doesn't travel as well as cream teas and Burberry raincoats.

Any visitor to Britain will soon discover that Muggeridge was right. The British are deadly serious about humor. In fact, the Brits are extremely *proud* of their sense of humor.

In the same way as you can divide society almost equally between those who love cats and those who love dogs, you can divide American society between those who find British humor and comedy

60

sidesplitting and those who find it so tedious and incomprehensible they'd rather spend the evening reading the Shanghai telephone book.

In dozens of families, one or more members watch every episode of *Are You Being Served?* or *Fawlty Towers* whilst others in the family would prefer peeling potatoes.

And, of course, the reverse is true. I am totally baffled by some of the comedy I see on American TV. Johnny Carson's sortie into the world of British television was a complete flop. I don't see what is so hilarious about *Murphy Brown* and *Roseanne* bores me to tears. On the other hand, *Cheers* and the *Golden Girls* had me in stitches. They have a devoted following in Britain.

People who speak North American English or British English share a common language and can generally understand each other. However, there is vocabulary, terminology, idioms and grammar rules unique to each version of the language despite the advances in mass communication of recent years. Humor and comedy are rooted in everyday experiences, attitudes and national characteristics.

Brits use points of reference from their culture - often not shared across the Pond. It is erroneous to assume what makes Britons laugh will also make Americans laugh - and vice-versa.

For example, a simple joke in Britain using wordplay. "How did the woman get over the 20-foot wall?" Answer: "She had a ladder in her stocking." This may raise a faint smile in a British audience but Americans may be baffled. They would use the word "run" not "ladder."

Americans will not understand jokes about Max Bygraves and Des O'Connor or Michael Heseltine just as Brits fail to comprehend gags about K-Mart or the IRS. Political satire may work on both sides of the Atlantic but only if it involves matters of international significance or refers to a well-known figure. Jokes about internal domestic issues meet with consternation.

Then there are the accents. Britons have trouble understanding one another's regional accents so how can Americans understand the broad speech of a Yorkshire comedy club or a Cockney pub? Much of the humor of Mr. Mash, the Cockney janitor in *Are You Being Served?* is wasted on an American audience because of the thickness of his accent. On the other hand, the Yiddish banter of Jackie Gleason is lost on all but a few British ears.

Adding to the difficulty for Americans trying to understand British humor are the odd traits of understatement and self-deprecation.

The Brits rarely say exactly what they mean, in fact they frequently say the opposite of what they mean. Members of the Opposition parties heaped lavish praise upon Margaret Thatcher when she bowed out of her premiership. Yet, during her tenure as prime minister she was the target of some of the most vitriolic comments ever made. What were the true feelings?

The British have a tremendous capacity to poke fun at themselves. Most Americans wouldn't dream of doing that. Poking fun at Britain - by Britons - is part of the national culture. With so much material it is done very well.

More seriously minded Americans, who are horrified when the flag is burned, find this way of life hard to fathom. For the British, humor is a way of letting their hair down in a manner transcending barriers of ethnicity, social or economic background. The British perception of America is of a nation that works too hard and takes itself a little bit too seriously. The Brits excel in seeing the funny side of unfortunate situations, including the great taboo, death.

I've divided British humor into six major categories, aspects of which can be found in all types of humor - literary, sitcom, stand-up and spoof.

1. The obsession with death.

In Britain, death is nothing to be afraid of, just laughed at. It is going to happen anyway. There's nothing anyone can do about it. The *Fawlty Towers* episode entitled *The Kipper and the Corpse* epitomizes the laissez faire attitude toward death. The death of a hotel guest in his room and Basil Fawlty's attempts to hide the body is a classic of British comedy. A good death or funeral joke always raises a laugh. Monty Python's most beloved skit - at least in Britain - is the one about the dead parrot.

2. The "put down."

Much of British comedy depends on the "put down" - ridiculing people in misfortune, those who are different or those regarded as "not normal." Putting down others is not a trait totally confined to the British. However, in a class ridden society with so many regional and ethnic variations, it provides more material than most countries.

For example, precisely the same jokes told about Poles in the US are told about the Irish. Plump people, foreigners (especially the Irish), effeminate gays, bald men, mothers-in-law are all seen as fair game. Political correctness may be in vogue, but in practice, it rarely gets in the way of a good, old belly laugh.

The best form of defense in Britain (and one that will earn you the deepest respect) is to poke fun at yourself, too.

3. Satire and spoof.

This form of comedy, though hardly confined to the British, has become one in which they excel. Television programs make fun of politicians, the government of the day, the Church, the Establishment - in fact, the entire British way of life. In the 1980s, a puppet show called *Spitting Image* satired everyone who was anyone, including the Queen. "Private Eye" is a magazine that continues to mock both the famous and not so famous, despite being sued over and over again.

4. Slapstick

Slapstick is the fodder of children's pantomimes but adults revel in it, too. It is a universal form of comedy. Note that Britains most successful comedy imports include some degree of slapstick, silly costumes and highly exaggerated characterizations.

5. Word-play, puns and innuendo.

Frequently used in British humor, they can be traced back to Saxon times when the English language was developing a strong oral tradition. Television comedy programs such as *Two Ronnies*, specialized in skits using word-play such as the "spoonerism."

In a line from a well-known comedy show, two chefs are deciding what to serve at a dinner party. "Let's give them roast centipede" says one. "It doesn't taste as good as turkey but at least everyone gets a leg."

6. Double *entendre.*

Perhaps Britain's most common and popular form of comedy is the double meaning or *double entendre*. It is the basic fodder of many stand-up comedians and television comedy shows - not to mention conversational humor.

It is hard for foreigners to understand much of it because of the differences in vocabulary. Much of it is sexual or lavatory innuendo. The *Carry On* films of the 1960s are a classic example - they are still being shown on TV. Benny Hill was a master of the double entendre.

Double *entendre* has a vocabulary all its own, frequently referring to parts of the human anatomy. When Benny Hill asked someone if so and so has a big one, we all know he is not asking about his house.

One day, I was on my way to a hotel where I was to be staying during an interview. I was carrying a newly dry-cleaned suit over my left arm. As I walked along the busy shopping street, a woman's voice called out for all to hear, "Excuse me, you've dropped your trousers."

She realized what she'd said and we started laughing. Soon the whole street was laughing with us.

7. The weather.

When all is said and done, perhaps the most significant contribution to British comedy is the weather. When it rains every day for a month, what else is there to do but laugh?

One of the greatest traits an individual - and a nation - can have is the ability to laugh at oneself.

Chapter Eight

HOLIDAYS AND LEISURE

" If all the year were playing holidays/To sport would be as tedious as work. "
William Shakespeare, *Henry IV*, Part 1

The British take their leisure time seriously. People will scrimp and save for months, even years, to make the most of their time off. Whether they plan a cottage on the Isle of Wight or a world cruise, Brits enjoy their holidays.

Low cost package tours have brought continental holiday locations within the grasp of multitudes of Brits. They can be seen soaking up the sun on the golden beaches of Majorca, Corfu - even Florida. "You get better fish and chips here" said one lobster red woman.

More than 90% of British workers are entitled to four weeks vacation a year. This is a big improvement from the early 1960s when 97% of the working population only received two weeks or less. Time off is calculated in weeks, not days, so weekends are not included in the calculation. Vacationing Brits (about 60%) take a break away from home of at least four nights.

In addition to vacation time, public holidays are sprinkled throughout the year. (Other European countries have more holidays than Britain.)

Most workers average 35-40 hours per week on their jobs. Saturdays and Sundays are the usual days off. Saturdays are reserved as a day for shopping, playing or watching sports. Sundays used to be a day for a "lie-in," washing the car or taking the kids out for the afternoon. With the liberalization of the Sunday trading laws, Sunday is fast becoming the most popular shopping day of the week.

The new laws are hotly contested by churches and unions fearful of worker exploitation and many small shops remain closed Sunday.

As Britain becomes increasingly multi-cultural, you will find shops and businesses belonging to members of ethnic communities closed on other days. For example, stores in the predominately Jewish suburb of Golder's Green in North London are mostly closed on Saturdays. In sections of those midland and northern cities with a large Muslim population, their shops are closed on Fridays.

British families spend around 16% of their household monies on leisure. Much of it is home-based. Close to 95% of households own a television set. They spend an average of twenty-five hours a week gawping at the box. Well over 50% of those whom own a television set also own videos *(VCRs)*.

Other popular leisure activities include listening to the radio, reading, DIY *(Do-It-Yourself)*, sports - both participatory and spectator, and, of course, gardening.

Britons own close to seven million dogs and seven million cats.

Approximately one-quarter of the population is involved in some kind of volunteer work.

Gambling is a popular pastime. Betting shops *(bookies)* are found in every shopping street. The shops specialize in, but are by no means confined to, horse racing. Bookies may offer bets involving a variety of popular issues ranging from who is likely to be the next Archbishop of Canterbury to which team will win the national soccer league. Vast sums of money are involved.

Another popular form of gambling is bingo, especially among the older people. Huge bingo halls can be found in towns and cities all over the country. They are usually owned by leisure chains such as Ladbrokes.

Equally popular is "the pools." Participants receive special forms on which they can predict the outcome of the following week's soccer games. Prizes are often in the millions of pounds.

Last, but not least, is the National Lottery. It is the brainchild of John Major's Conservative government. Millions of Britons participate every week. The first prize reaches well into the millions of pounds. Much of the money raised by the lottery is plowed back into community projects at both the national and local levels.

Christmas - even if you are not an adherent of the Christian faith - is the main time for families and friends to get together. The Christmas hype begins around mid-October. Commercials advertising the latest toys appear on TV. Tinsel and Christmas trees appear in shops and stores. You can hear the angels singing, "Glory to God in the High." Christmas cribs *(creches)* appear all over the country without objections. Special Christmas illuminations grace the main shopping areas of the major town and cities creating a festive atmosphere.

Despite advancing secularity, Christmas as a religious feast manages to persevere. Religious teaching is compulsory in British schools. A morning religious assembly is legally a part of every school program. Religious observances such as carol services, Christmas pageants or plays are presented before the end of the semester. Thousands of first and second graders parade in nativity costumes and plastic baby-doll Jesus's appear all over the country.

In the home, they put decorations up any time between December 1 and Christmas Eve. Generally more gaudy than American Christmas trees, the green of the fake (occasionally real) tree is barely visible under the tinsel, flashing fairy lights and shimmering baubles.

During the season, carol singers make a fortune doing the rounds of neighborhood streets and pub. However, it's all for a good cause. Charities such as

Save the Children and Oxfam are among the main beneficiaries. It's much like a Dickensian street - except for the electric lamps, passing cars and absence of snow.

Planning for Christmas Day starts early in homes. In Britain, Christmas Day is like the American and Canadian Thanksgiving Day in that it is the only time of the year when family members make a real effort to get together. The media puts out constant reminders that this is the season of goodwill to all. This is to offset family squabbles about who will have Aunt Maud this year.

December 26 is Boxing Day. Also a public holiday, it gives people ample time to recover.

The Sunday before Christmas many Anglican (Church of England-Episcopal) parishes will hold a traditional service of *Nine Lessons and Carols* modeled on the King's College, Cambridge original. Sometimes it is a candlelight ceremony.

Christmas Eve, many churches have a Children's Service in the late afternoon or early evening with a Midnight Communion (or Midnight Mass) later on. More adventurous congregations have been known to follow their midnight service with a glass of mulled wine and a mince pie. Others keep the wretched pies secure in rector's fridge until after the morning service on Christmas Day. Then they are consumed with a glass of cream sherry.

Meanwhile, the children are sleeping poorly -

especially those in a modern home with no chimney. Years ago, Bing Crosby taught British kids who Santa Claus is but they still prefer to call him Father Christmas. Parents set out a glass of cream sherry and a mince pie for Saint Nick to keep him going through his arduous night's work. Both pie and sherry miraculously disappear by morning.

For families with children, Christmas Day begins with the opening of presents which mysteriously appeared during the night.

In up market families, including the royal one, children may have to wait until after the traditional lunch of turkey, duck, pheasant or some other bird, stuffing, Brussels sprouts, parsnips, crispy roast potatoes, red currant sauce and gravy.

All this is followed by a heavy pudding. In a quaint British custom, the pudding is doused with brandy and set afire. The life threatening fire is put out with an equally life threatening rich, custard sauce. When eating the pudding people with weak or false teeth should be on guard because the pudding traditionally contains a coin (it used to be sixpence before decimalization). The coin is supposed to bring good luck to the person who finds it - or bad luck, one assumes, to the person who swallows it.

A nifty table decoration enhances the scene. Brightly colored Christmas Crackers are at each individual's place at the table. Most are a paper tube about six inches long with twisted ends. They contain gunpowder and are pulled with your immediate neighbor at the table in tug-o-war style. The resultant loud banging noise is enough to wake up snoozing, old Aunt Maud. As the cracker is further dismantled, a small gift and a brightly colored, flimsy paper crown pops out. It is customary to wear your crown all day unless, like Her Majesty, you are wearing a real one.

Speaking of Her Majesty, the entire country stops eating at 3:00 P.M. to watch the Queen's Christmas Speech on TV. This custom began with George V's radio broadcast.

After a period of snoozing - possible prompted by the speech or more likely because Aunt Maud insists on watching *The Sound of Music* on BBC1, the next highlight of the day is more eating - usually cold meat and other leftovers with pickles and the like.

The good news is tomorrow being Boxing Day, it's another day off. By the time you've really recovered - it's New Years Eve! This holiday is another excuse for revelry. The romantically inclined may attend a dinner dance. The young may celebrate at the local pub or disco. Perhaps a boozy evening with members of your calling circle or watching TV specials featuring kilt-clad singers and bagpipes may be the choice.

At midnight on New Year's Eve, huge crowds gather in Trafalgar Square, London and in city centers all over the country to listen for Big Ben (its chimes carry very well). Wherever you are, it is customary to join arms with those around you and sing a chorus of *Auld Lang Syne.*

January 1 is, thankfully, a national holiday in England, Scotland and Wales. New Year's Eve is celebrated with exceptional intensity in Scotland, where it is called *Hogmanay.*

They observe St. Valentine's Day in Britain. Millions of anonymous cards are mailed to sweethearts. In national and local newspapers, a plethora of "To my darling Piggy-Wiggy" style Valentine messages appear in the classified sections.

Pre-Lenten activities are widely observed. Britain's somewhat less colorful equivalent of the *Mardi Gras* celebrations in Rio and New Orleans are the Shrove Tuesday Pancake Races. These are held all over the country. The contestants are usually local homemakers. They race a hundred yards or so while holding in one hand a frying pan containing a pancake. They must toss the pancake a specified number of times during the race.

The practice of making pancakes is derived from the custom of using up all the fat in the household before Lent. The day before Ash Wednesday is called both Fat Tuesday and Shrove Tuesday. The word "shrove" is the past tense of an old English verb "to shrive." People would come to church before Lent to be shriven of their sins before Ash Wednesday.

Good Friday is a national public holiday in

England and Wales but not in Scotland. For most people, its religious significance is not marked by attendance in church but by the consumption of hot cross buns. Religious presentations dominate the serious radio stations and there is a glut of religious programs on TV. Until fairly recently, most shops and stores remained closed out of respect for the day. Today, many shops and businesses remain open.

Easter Day is a time for family get-togethers - though not to the same extent as Christmas. Lamb with mint sauce is a traditional favorite for lunch. The children in a family are not likely to be feeling hungry since they have probably been gorging themselves on huge chocolate eggs - the customary gift for them on this day. In England, Easter Monday is a public holiday.

The last Monday in May is also a public holiday in England. This is a day when people take the opportunity to get out of the house for a few hours, preferably to the seaside. In Scotland, the only fixed public holiday is January 1 but all Scottish towns and cities have a one-day holiday in both Spring and Fall. They are usually on Mondays.

Much mirth is generated on April 1 - April Fool's Day. The mischief extends to nationally respect newspapers - even the BBC! One year a circus clown appeared during one of the BBC's prime time news broadcasts. On another occasion, during a serious news broadcast, they announced that an

75

unidentified flying object had landed in Hyde Park. Hundreds of people made their way to the park to investigate only to discover it was and April Fool hoax.

Unlike North America where Mother's Day is largely the result of blatant commercialism, Britain's *Mothering Sunday* is traditionally observed on the middle Sunday of Lent. (The media misname it Mother's Day). It is one of the best Sundays of the year for church attendance. An emphasis is placed on children's participation. Many churches hand out gifts - usually daffodils - for children to give to their mothers. They buy cards and TV commercials advertise gifts so there is a commercial aspect to the observance. Nevertheless, it is not the big deal it is in the US.

Britons with families tend to take their vacations during the school summer holidays. These start around the beginning of July to early September. British seaside resorts and other tourist attractions are extremely busy and do the bulk of their trade during this time. Roads and motorways, especially those leading to and from the coast, become clogged with huge traffic jams miles long.

The summer holiday season in England and Wales culminates on the August Bank Holiday. They assume it this will be a "washout" day even if the weather has been good for weeks. It always seems to rain on this holiday but that doesn't stop Brits from heading for the beach.

Like Labor Day in the U.S., August Bank Holiday Monday marks the end of the official summer season. However, if the weather is good, crowds will descend on the coast until well into September and even October. Excepting Christmas and Boxing Day, this is the last public holiday of the year.

Moving on through the year, another popular occasion drawing large attendances to church is Harvest Thanksgiving Sunday. This celebration has it roots in Britain's agricultural past. They usually observe it around September 29 though it has no fixed date. This is the feast day of St. Michael and All Angels, abbreviated to Michaelmas.

They decorate churches with fruits, vegetables and even canned goods - filling every windowsill. Specially decorated loaves of bread adorn the altar. Afterwards, these goods are often packaged and given to the poor. The occasion is rarely marked except for church services.

Halloween has grown in popularity in recent years, thanks to the influence of Hollywood. It is still overshadowed by November 5, the anniversary of the day in 1605 when a certain Guy Fawkes attempted to blow up parliament along with King James I.

Guy Fawkes Night - also called Firework Night is observed with the lighting of bonfires and the setting off of fireworks in individual gardens. Increasingly, given the danger of burns, the fires and fireworks are in community-sponsored displays.

Before the day, children make a Guy - an effigy wearing Dad's old clothes. They parade it on the street and ask passers-by to "donate a penny for the Guy." Typically, the donations received go towards the purchase of fireworks.

In a practice every bit as horrendous as anything observed on Halloween, they burn the effigy on a bonfire. This custom dates back to the anti-Catholic sentiment following the original Gunpowder Plot. It is actively discouraged by the now friendly religious denominations.

Remembrance Sunday is the day war veterans all over the nation give thanks for the sacrifice of "so many for so few" during the First and Second World Wars and other subsequent conflicts. Religious and secular ceremonies are held on the Sunday nearest November 11th. (The treaty ending World War I was signed on November 11, 1918.)

The nation's principal act of remembrance is held at the Cenotaph (war memorial) in Whitehall, London. It is usually attended by the Sovereign and other dignitaries and is televised nationally.

Smaller scale commemorations are held in virtually every town and village. Veterans march proudly through the streets.

Also, around this time, large sections of the population wear bright, red paper poppies in their buttonholes as a sign of respect for those who died.

Most ceremonies are marked by a moving rendition of the *Last Post and Reveille*. Remembrance Sunday took on an added poignancy in 1995 when the fiftieth anniversary of the ending of World War II was observed.

Americans in Britain on Thanksgiving may feel quite homesick since this is not an observed holiday in the country. Some central London and Edinburgh hotels put on special meals for U.S. expatriates. They are often expensive. Some American restaurants in Britain also serve Thanksgiving meals.

The British, especially the English, don't go in for much patriotic fervor except in one time situations. The commemorations to mark the 50th anniversary of the end of World War II was one such special occasion. Homes were draped in Union flags and street parties were held the length and breadth of the country.

The Union flag - commonly called the Union Jack - commands respect but is not afforded the status bordering on reverence the Stars and Stripes enjoys in the U.S. As in the U.S., a code of etiquette for flying the British flag exists but they rarely enforce it. Purists complain the flag frequently flies upside down - even in public places.

Virtually no one flies the Union Flag from a mast in their yard (few have yards that are big enough.) Britons are more likely to purchase Union Jack underwear or paint it on their ceilings. And while few approve of burning the Flag, even in protest, they won't get upset if someone does - unless they're French.

The Scots and the Welsh take more pride in their identity than the English do in theirs. Perhaps this is not surprising given the fact that for centuries they have been swamped with the Anglo-Saxon culture. St. Andrew's Day on November 30 and Robbie Burns night, January 25 are both occasions for national pride and pageantry in Scotland. All good Welshmen and women wear a daffodil on St. David's Day, April 1. While England's St. George's Day (April) passes without so much as a whimper.

SECTION TWO

SYSTEMS

Chapter Nine

TRANSPORTATION

"The driving is like the driving of Jehu, the son of Nimshi; for he driveth furiously."
                                        Bible: Kings 9:20

Travel by Car

Great Britain, away from its clogged up conurbations, is ideal for a driving vacation for several good reasons:

▶ You can explore off-the-beaten path locations untouched by train or bus.

▶ The comforting fact that you can scratch your nose or kiss your loved one in relative privacy.

▶ You can pull into a roadside restaurant for a meal or to use the loo.

▶ The freedom to stop at a whim to photograph a stunning Lakeland landscape or a herd of grazing New Forest ponies.

Note: Don't let the quaint British habit of driving on the left deter you. It is said to be part of history - originating with the Roman legions' habit of marching on the left-hand side of roads.

Whatever your reasons for driving:

▶ You must *always* have a valid U.S. or

Canadian driver's license on you.

- ▸ . You must have proper insurance coverage.
- ▸ Be sure you understand the workings of your car before you begin to drive it.
- ▸ A good sized car is essential.
- ▸ Secure and read a copy of the *Highway Code* - available at just about every bookstore and newsagent in the United Kingdom.

Although comfortable buses run frequently and trains are faster and more luxurious than ever, something can be said for traveling from A to B without the necessity of entrusting the first and last five miles of your journey to taxi, local bus or worst of all, walking in those three inch stilettos.

Many Americans visiting Britain for the first time want to "do" the entire country in a week. Technically, that is possible. After all, the nation is one third the size of Texas and about the same size as New York. Visitors soon find, however, that Britain's population is three times that of Texas and four times that of New York. At certain times of the day, all 60 million inhabitants (plus tourists) seem to be out on the road at the same time. The result is long lines, *jams* or *snarl-ups* curtailing progress considerably.

For those who want to travel quickly from one end of the country to the other (more than 868 miles from John o' Groats in Scotland to Land's End in Cornwall) use the *fairly* reliable system of motorways

("fairly" because motorways such as the M1 and M6 seem to be in a constant state of repair - with consequent traffic jams.)

For those who want to concentrate on one or two counties or regions, the "A" roads (the main roads before the arrival of motorways) and the "B" roads are almost universally well-surfaced and in good shape.

Unclassified roads - predominately very pretty but often narrow country lanes used by farmers and other quaint country folk - are also well surfaced usually. They may have unconventional hazards such as herds of goats, cows or sheep blocking the way for long periods.

Traffic priorities (rights of way) are clearly established and indicated on British roads. For example, approaching a continuous white line at an intersection means you must come to a complete stop, while a *fragmented* (dashed) line means *give way* (yield). Road signs conform to international standards. They are clear and easily understood.

Driving in Britain is expensive. Quite apart from the exorbitant cost of renting a car, (do your homework before you leave home) government taxes on petrol (gasoline) make it as much as four times more expensive than gasoline in the U.S. or Canada. Gas prices at the roadside are given in liters only. Keep your calculator handy. Of course, the more passengers you have in the car, the cheaper the relative cost.

All new cars sold in Britain use only unleaded gas but many older cars still on the road using leaded gas can make busy city streets overpoweringly smelly.

Unlike the U.S. where a complicated and varying ritual must be performed before the gas is released from the pump, pumping gas in Britain is simple. Drive up to the pump, unlock and remove your gas cap (British gas tanks nearly always have a key - so precious are their contents.) Then, insert the hose and start pumping - no levers to turn or switches to flick.

Driving a car in the land of hope and glory is as easy as steak and kidney pie once you have mastered basic, logical steps. Some of them are peculiar to Britain, some are common sense anywhere you drive.

If you are the driver:

▸ Don't drink or use drugs and drive.

▸ Read the *Highway Code* before starting.

▸ Drive on the left and therefore sit on the right. Getting in and out of the car on the correct side will take some getting used to.

▸ *Overtake* (pass) only on the right.

▸ Use your left hand to manipulate the shift. Most British cars have a manual shift. Avoid this added complication by specifying automatic transmission when you rent the car.

▸ Look in the mirror to your left, not right.

86

- On the motorway, keep to left lane unless passing. Never switch from lane to lane unless passing, instructed to do so by police or signs.
- Turning right at a red light is not allowed.
- Always stop for pedestrians in a *zebra* (striped) zone. Give them priority at the times shown in the Highway Code.
- Do not drive when you are extremely tired or suffering from jet lag. During the first few days of your visit, take it easy. Short, leisurely drives will ease you into new driving routines.

The foot controls in British cars are in the same positions as in U.S. vehicles. From left to right are the clutch, brake and gas.

Driving problems are minimal with normal driving but they may appear when panic sets in. The car stalls and in a split second you look up to the right for the mirror and it's not there. You automatically reach to the right for the shift and it's not there. You eventually get started and drive off, only to find a thirty-ton articulated truck coming straight at you. You are driving on the wrong side of the road - again. Hopefully the driver sees you in time. If not, expect *at least* a few hours delay in getting to your destination.

It may take two or three days to get used to driving on the left but even later, ten days or two weeks into your vacation, you will still find yourself occasionally glancing up at a nonexistent mirror or reaching for a nonexistent shift.

Americans sometimes experience culture shock driving on country roads in Britain. They claim these are narrower and more curvy than roads back home. They are! In the U.S. a road from one place to another is usually direct. In Britain, if a pretty rose bush is in the way of a proposed new "relief" road, they hold a public enquiry and build the road around it.

Brits drive fast. The national speed limit is 70 MPH. Get used to the fact that even on wafer thin country roads you're likely to be passed at 80 MPH by nonagenarian ladies in their half-timbered Austin 1100s or Morris Minors. Watch out for motorists passing you even when you are doing 90! Brits have an infuriating habit of attempting to pass on narrow country lanes only five feet wide. Do not attempt to copy them; it is an art that takes years to master. Why be suicidal just to save a few minutes driving time?

Driving in cities presents some problems, too. Residential roads can prove lethal for an inexperienced driver. Already narrow, busy thoroughfares may seem even narrower with cars parked on both sides. It looks as if a camel could get through the eye of a needle more easily than you can get to end of the street. Be on guard for car doors opening, wobbly cyclists (who are probably even more scared than you are), and large single or double-decker buses moving off without signaling.

Proceed with caution. Do not allow yourself to

be intimidated or provoked by impatient local drivers rushing home to watch the latest episode of *East Enders* on BBC1.

Another problem area for foreign drivers is the *roundabout* (traffic circles a central spot). A roundabout may cover an area as large a several football *pitches* (fields). The Marble Arch roundabout in London, for example. Or it can be as simple as a car tire stuck in the center of a busy crossroads. Often the larger ones are disarmingly pretty, planted with geraniums, *rockeries* (rock gardens), waterfalls and flowering shrubs. Sometimes roundabouts encompass entire public parks such as Piccadilly Plaza in Manchester.

Attempting to circle a roundabout counterclockwise is easy for a driver unaccustomed to driving on the left. This action can have serious consequences for what may be left of your car - and *you*. Watch the traffic and think before you enter.

Traffic on a roundabout always has *priority* (right-of-way) unless expressly indicated otherwise. When entering a roundabout, wait at the line until you see a space, then go. Be sure to *indicate* (signal) when exiting. Tourists have been known to go round and round the circle because they don't know how to use the roundabout properly. Roundabouts work pretty well and help keep traffic flowing if they are respected.

Whatever you do, *don't stop in a roundabout*

to photograph the pretty flowers.

It makes good sense to buy - and read - a copy of the *Highway Code* if you are going to be driving in the U.K. Her Majesty's Stationery Office, no less, produces it. Within its pages you will find explanations of street signs, driving regulations and much more. It is available at most bookshops.

The pub is still a popular institution and being drunk in public is only marginally less fashionable than it used to be, but drinking alcohol and driving are definite no-nos. Expect no mercy from the police if they catch you over the limit. Even if you are in an accident that is not your fault, if you are drunk according to law, be prepared for stiff fines.

The wearing of front seat belts is compulsory throughout Great Britain. They require wearing back seat belts in all cars where they are provided. Young children must be in special children's seats. Again, the law of the land imposes stiff fines for failure to abide.

Americans are surprised by the large numbers of Brits who do not drive. Until recently driving a car was not necessary for people living in cities and towns. Shopping was done locally in a suburban high street or downtown area. People shopped on foot or used one of the frequent bus services. Visits farther afield usually meant using the train. Even today, with such and efficient bus and train system, using a car in central London and other large cities is a crazy waste of time, money and energy.

Until Conservative transport minister Dr. Beeching cut rail service in the 1960s, virtually every town in Britain with a population of 5,000 or more had train service.

Now, as in America, the car rules supreme. Quite shortsightedly, more and more out-of-town shopping malls, drive-in restaurants, movie theatres and even drive-on trains for the Channel Tunnel are being constructed. Some cynics call it the "Americanization" of Britain. Whatever you call it, the truth is that Britain's road arteries are clogging rapidly and the old girl is heading for a serious stroke - with paralysis.

It is a tragedy that British politicians have failed to learn from America's mistakes. Revitalized downtowns, large-scale investment in railroads and other public transportation schemes such as those being planned in many U.S. cities at this time will not only result in a more pleasant lifestyle but in a safer, cleaner environment for everyone.

You will find most of British are polite, cautious drivers. With many more cars per inch on the roads than in either the U.S. or Canada, driving in Britain (for the British, at least) is safer than driving in America.

If you *should* be involved in an accident, exchange insurance information with the other driver just as you do in the U.S. Call the police for anything but the most minor of fender benders.

Train Travel

It has happened. One of Britain's greatest public assets, the nationalized British Rail is no more. They have sold it off, divided it up and replaced it by a complex mishmash of smaller companies. Each company owns and operates a specific aspect of the system, such as rolling stock, track, catering and so on.

The self-deprecating Brits regarded poking fun at BR as a national pastime. Whole books could be filled with jokes about the dubious nature of its timekeeping, the quality of its rolling stock and the flavor of its tea. The jokes can be traced to the savage butchery of the system in the 1960's. The Conservative Government of the time wiped out many loss-making rural lines in one fell swoop.

Other jokes owe their existence to what seemed like an endless series of rail strikes in the 1970s and 1980s led by the powerful National Union of Railway men.

Even thinned down and only a mere shadow of its former glory, BR was a precious gem providing (generally) fast, efficient services between major centers of population, stopping at many smaller towns along the way. What was good enough for Miss Marple and Hercule Poirot should have been left intact.

In recent years, many profitable lines were spruced up beyond recognition - primarily to encourage potential investors. New rolling stock replaced the medieval carriages so familiar in the 60s and 70s. They replaced old tracks with continuously welded track allowing smoother, faster journeys - up to 140 mph on some routes. Many major stations, such as Waterloo in London, have been renovated and now rival the Chelsea Flower Show with their floral displays and Covent Garden for their cafes and restaurants.

The audio equipment was improved - now you can even understand what the announcer is saying! Thousands of pounds were spent teaching the British Rail staff how to smile and say, "please" and "thank you." (They drew the line at saying, "Have a nice day.")

It would be naive to believe all this has been done simply to provide better service for tourists, commuters and others. British Rail, nationalized by the Labour Government of 1947, had been close to the top of the Conservative government's list for privatization.

With much of the money to finance the improvements coming from long suffering passengers rather than direct government subsidy, fares are exceedingly high and show every sign of increasing under privatization.

The fares structure, already complicated

beyond belief in British Rail's time, almost requires a college degree to work out. Most tourists become utterly confused and bewildered. As with the airways, much hinges on *when* you journey. Off-peak travel costing less and first-class costing the most. Day *returns* (round trips) provide the best deal. It works something like this: a *single* (one-way) ticket from Bournemouth to London costs £24. A "period return" would allow a few days in the capital, would cost £27; a *day return*(coming back the same day) costs the same as the single fare. First class fares are higher, of course.

In most European countries, travelling by rail is one of the most satisfying, relaxing ways of seeing a country. You will meet people, see some beautiful scenery - as well as its grottiest suburbs. "Letting the train take the strain" in Britain has always been a great way to travel. Time will tell if the newly privatized companies can deliver the kind of service that British Rail was able to provide

Do your homework to take the best advantage of train travel in Britain.

Note: Buy a BritRail pass before you travel. You are not able to buy them in Britain. Check with your travel agent or call 888-BRITRAIL.

Note: You can now travel from London to Paris in about three hours on the train.

Buses and Coaches

When you hear the word "bus" in Britain it usually means local or regional service operated by private companies or, sometimes, by local authorities. The bus service is comprehensive with frequent runs of single or double-decker buses along many main urban routes.

Local buses are numbered for identification both front and back. Usually you pay-as-you-enter, though some lines still have conductors who will come around to collect your fare. Fares are usually calculated on the basis of distance travelled though some places operate on a flat fare basis.

Bus stops are clearly marked. You may have to hold out your hand as a signal for the bus to stop for you.

Local bus rides are good places to meet the regional people. Show interest in the things you see and you will soon have someone - or several someones - telling you all about them!

Be aware that services may be slow and erratic during peak traffic, despite specially marked bus lanes. This may prompt jokes like, "Why is the No. 23 route called the banana route? All the buses come in bunches."

Long distance buses are called "coaches" in Britain. A network of coaches links towns and cities operated by National Express or Scottish Citylink.

Coaches may not be as comfortable as trains, though many new models have toilets, refreshments and even color television. Coaches are not as fast as trains. The trip from London to Edinburgh takes eight hours on a coach but only four and one half hours on the fastest train but they are often less expensive, particularly if you can travel off peak times. Making reservations for coach travel is advisable.

The London Underground

Once you have mastered the technique of traveling the "Tube," you'll find it a great way of getting around London quickly.

Note: The morning and evening rush hours can be frightening when you are unfamiliar with the system. Commuters squeeze into trains as tightly as sardines in a can and the platforms look very narrow. Avoid traveling then if you can.

The London Underground system is the world's oldest. It covers the area north of the Thames comprehensively, especially the central area. (Surface rail provides most services south of the River.)

The Underground lines are tunneled at different levels and color-coded on the maps. Check to make sure that you are on the correct platform (northbound - southbound or eastbound - westbound). Check the destination on the front of the train and the electronic signboard before you board. Many lines split into two or three.

Make sure you have a valid ticket. *Single* (one-way) and *returns* (round-trip) tickets are available. A daily Travelcard may give you the best value for your money.

Travelers purchase tickets from machines or at the ticket office. Machines provide change if required. Insert your ticket into a slot at the turnstile. The gate opens for you to enter.

Be sure to pick up your ticket after you enter. When you reach your destination, you'll need it again to open the gate so you can get out. Then, if your ticket is no longer valid, the machine will gobble it up. If the ticket is valid for further use, the machine will return it to you.

Most stations have escalators for access to trains; some have *lifts* (elevators). The escalators are often very long.

Once you have mastered the basics, the system is fun to use.

Air Travel Within the U.K.

Given the comparatively small geographical area of the country, domestic air travel has never been as popular with Brits as other means of public transport. However, there is a network of regional airports besides the main international airports in London, Birmingham, Manchester and Glasgow.

Journeys rarely take longer than an hour and a half. There are frequent flights on the main routes to London, Edinburgh or Glasgow, but they can be pricey. Usually the best deals are tickets sold within seven days of departure. Bargain fares usually require staying over a Saturday night.

Domestic carriers include British Airways, British Midland, Air UK and LoganAir.

Note: A round trip in Britain is called a return. You will ask for a "London to Edinburgh return." A one-way trip is a single.

Planned air travel within Britain may be less expensive if you plan your itinerary and make reservations before you travel. Check with your travel agent.

Chapter Ten

EDUCATION

"Genius lasts longer than beauty. That accounts for the fact that we all take such pains to overeducate ourselves."
Oscar Wilde: Picture of Dorian Gray, 1891

At one time, education in Britain was the sole responsibility of the Church. The earliest schools were usually connected with the monastic communities and the teachers were usually monks. Education was limited to the sons of the aristocrats and the wealthy. Britain's ancient universities - Oxford and Cambridge in England (known collectively as Oxbridge) and St. Andrews in Scotland started out as religious foundations.

Considerable impetus was given to education during the Renaissance period. Many schools and colleges were established during the fifteenth and sixteenth centuries.

As more and more people earned the right to vote, so the demand for educational opportunities among the masses grew. Eventually the responsibility for education was assumed by the State. Education for boys and girls was made compulsory by a Parliamentary Act of 1870. Institutions known at first as "board" schools and later as "council" schools were set up alongside existing church establishments. Elementary education was distinguished from secondary. Technical education was introduced.

Old universities were reorganized and opened up to non-Episcopalians. New universities, called redbrick universities, were founded.

For the wealthy, the public school system was expanded. (In Britain, "public" school means private.)

In 1891, education in elementary schools was made free. Before that, fees had been paid according to the parents' income. By 1918, children could leave school at age 14. Now the school leaving age is 16.

All British children must be educated between the ages of five to sixteen. It is the parent's or guardian's responsibility to see this happens. Very few Britons educate their children at home. Some choose private education in either boarding or day schools for their children.

For most parents the choice is between the various schools provided in their district by the local education authority (LEA).

Except in London, where individual boroughs are the educational authority, The LEA is usually a county council, or in large urban areas, a metropolitan district council. It must offer a free place for each child from the beginning of the term following his or her fifth birthday. Sometimes it can offer a place sooner.

The following is an outline of the educational

system in England and Wales. Scotland has its own distinct system.

Elementary Education

Limited places are obtainable for children under five in state-run nursery schools or in primary schools (both free). There are privately run *playgroups* available for a fee.

After the nursery school, the child moves on to a Primary School, often divided between and Infant and Junior section. Parents have a degree of choice about which school they prefer for their child.

Around the age of eleven, a *Secondary School* must be chosen. A few areas have "middle" schools for children aged eight, nine and ten, then move on to Secondary School at age thirteen. They will complete their basic education there at age sixteen.

If a child decides to continue his or her education after age sixteen, he/she may stay on at the same secondary school or transfer to another school or sixth form college.

Many schools insist their pupils wear a school uniform. Children in matching uniforms are a familiar sight on any British city street. Many children live close enough to walk to school. Others living farther afield may use heavily subsidized scheduled public transport, special school buses or their parent's car.

Be aware while driving in Britain that school buses are considerably different from their American counterparts. To begin with, they are not painted yellow (except in Bournemouth). They may be either single or double-decker and may be poorly marked. In fact, British school buses vary in colour or size, depending on the vehicles the local bus company has available. The only way of telling school buses apart from the regularly scheduled services may be a small sign on the front and back - and the terrifying din, shouting and screaming emanating from within.

There are no red stop signs or flashing lights to warn you that children may be crossing the road.

Options

The majority of schools, known as *county* schools, are entirely the responsibility of the LEA. About a third of the schools in the country are known as *voluntary* schools. Their running costs are paid by LEAs. They usually have a distinctive character, often because they were founded by a religious body. In many of the voluntary schools elected or appointed governors, not the LEA, employ the staff and decide on which pupils to admit. They may have an agreement with the LEA to limit the number of pupils who are not adherents of their particular faith.

Most church schools, for example, implement a policy of offering places to children of the parish first. Secondly, to children from other same-denomination parishes and then to children of non-adherents living within the parish boundaries. Some secondary schools and a very few primary schools admit only children of the same sex.

In most areas, secondary schools are known as *comprehensives*. This means they admit pupils of all abilities. A small minority of local authorities maintain the old "grammar school" system. In this system, children of advanced academic achievement are siphoned off into grammar schools. The children not meeting the required admission standards for grammar schools attend *secondary modern* schools. The debate about the validity of comprehensive education rages on even today.

Parents deciding to send their child to a public (private) school will usually have to pay fees. In some public secondary schools, parents on lower incomes can get assistance towards fees from the Government's *Assisted Places* scheme.

Public (private) schools may be day schools or boarding schools.

Academic

A National Curriculum for all British schoolchildren was introduced by the Conservative government in 1989. It covers English, maths (math), science, design and technology, history, geography, a modern foreign language, art, music and physical education. The student must study up to age sixteen.

Appropriate arrangements are made for children with special education needs.

Religious education is included in the basic curriculum. Fifty percent must be Christian and there is supposed to be a daily religious act of worship. A child may choose not to attend. Other subjects, other than those listed here, may be studied.

A pupil's progress in subjects in the National Curriculum is measured against national standard in primary schools at the ages of seven and eleven and in secondary school at ages fourteen and sixteen. Assessments are made through a series of written and practical tests. Results of their tests at age fourteen will influence the choice of subjects the pupil will specialize in for the GCSE (General Certificate of Secondary Education). Many employees insist on a minimum of three GCSE passes in English, maths and science before they will consider an applicant.

GCSE grades, ranging from G up to A are awarded at the end of the two-year course. The awards are based on the assessment of course work as well as end-of-course exams.

TVEI stands for Technical and Vocational Education Initiative was another initiative by the last Conservative Government. It is not a qualification or examination. It is a means of providing extra money so that schools and colleges can make lessons more practical and relevant to adult life and work.

All secondary schools offer career advice. Local LEAs provide careers officers who work closely with schools in their jurisdiction. Some schools arrange work-experience placements. Visits from local employers to schools are frequently organized.

Decisions made at the age of sixteen are crucial. Young people in Britain can choose to leave school at that age. They can decide to stay on in full time education in school or college. They can go to a YTS (Youth Training Scheme) or find a job with training.

The main courses for those who choose to stay on in school are "A" (Advanced) and "AS" levels. Passing at least two "A" levels or four "AS" levels (Half the course work of an "A"level) is normally the minimum requirement for studying for a degree at universities, polytechnics and colleges of higher education. Even if a person is not going on to degree study, having a few "A" levels successfully completed can make a big difference when looking for a job.

A student in Britain has many job-related courses available, leading to qualifications directly related to a career. Subjects range from engineering an computing to textiles, printing and hairdressing. The courses generally include work-experience. They are usually offered by recognized professional bodies, regional examining boards and individual colleges.

CPVEs are Certificates of Prevocational training offered to sixteen year olds who have not decided on a particular career. The course is normally one year in duration. It offers the person the chance to gain skills and practical work-experience in a variety of work areas. Achievements are recorded in a nationally recognized certificate.

School life in Britain does not end with a prom. Thank God!

Further Education

When a sixteen year old's choice is to continue studying, then the next decision is where to go - a school or college. The choice may be determined by the courses offered, the reputation and facilities of the institution and transportation.

School *sixth forms* tend to concentrate on the more academic "A" and "AS" courses. *Further Education Colleges* provide a wide range of job-related classes as well as "A" levels.

The YTS is a two-year program. It offers the opportunity to experience different types of work in a work place. Every trainee has the chance to earn a job-related qualification or a credit toward one.

Higher Education

When Brits ask, "Where did you go to school?" they *never* mean higher education. "School" is used to describe only those establishments attended from ages five through sixteen.

Most of the newer British universities are located on purpose-built campuses. Some of the older institutions are more spread out, often covering a large proportion of the downtown area with individual colleges or faculties. Oxford and Cambridge are examples of how the old institutions become part of the town.

Most undergraduates choose a "single honours" degree. The work is concentrated primarily in one area of study. "Majoring" is only relevant when "combined honours" degrees are sought.

Each college, polytechnic or university issues a detailed annual prospectus. Subjects offered are listed along with other information about attractions such as sports and social activities. Well before completing "A" or "AS" levels, a student writes off for the prospectuses of various institutions and studies them.

The student fills in an application form listing five universities, in order of preference, details of their requested course of study and other relevant information. The application is sent to UCCA (the University Central Council on Admissions). They forward the information about the candidate to the five universities specified. Each university contacts the candidate to inform them what "A" and "AS" level passes and grades are required to gain admission.

Certain universities, particularly those who regard themselves as the "Ivy League" of Britain, will ask for very high grades in at least one subject. This may not be the same subject the person desires to study. Some universities may also insist on a personal interview.

When the "A" and "AS" level results are published in July, the candidates will know whether or not they have been accepted at any of the five desired institutions.

A place may be available at another institution not previously considered if a student's grade is not as high as that required by any of the applied for five universities.

Polytechnics work in much the same way except they are heavily biased towards the sciences.

Term time begins in late September or early October. For the first week or so, the entering students will be known as *fresher*s (not freshmen). Once the novelty of being a fresher wears off, the student is called simply "first-year." Second year is known as exactly that (The word "sophomore" means absolutely nothing to the average Brit.) Third year students are surprisingly known as "third-years."

Most first degree courses last for three years. They include assessment and examinations and result in a bachelor's degree. The credit system is not generally used.

After the degree is awarded, the student may continue to study at the same place - or elsewhere - for a master's degree. This study involves the writing of a thesis with guidance from academic staff or regular examinations. The student may go on for a doctorate.

Higher education in Britain (for British citizens) is generally free. Candidates from wealthy families may have to contribute toward the costs of tuition and accommodations. Less well off young people may have this paid for. In addition, they may qualify for additional funding by the Government working through the LEA. Financing for post-graduate degrees tends to come from the individual or an institution.

Students may live in their own homes, university owned halls of residence, student villages or in private homes in the neighbourhood.

Social activities are provided by the individual department of study and by the Students' Union. In most cases, the Students' Unions are affiliated with the National Union of Students. One of the highlights of student life (and the bane of local residents) is "Rag Week." This is an entire week set aside for charitable fund-raising - often of a questionable nature.

With emphasis on academic achievement rather than financial capability, a smaller proportion of British young people traditionally attended high education than their American and Canadian counterparts. In 1990 there were forty universities in Britain. By 1995 government policy towards higher education was changing. Twenty new universities were established. Purists see this as the beginning of a slippery slide in academic standards. Only time will tell.

Chapter Eleven

CRIME AND PUNISHMENT

"Is there any point to which you would wish to draw my attention?"
"To the curious incident of the dog in the night-time."
"The dog did nothing in the night-time."
"That was the curious incident." remarked Sherlock Holmes

While America was rivetted by the trial of O.J. Simpson, Britain was spellbound by the trial of Frederick and Rosemary West. They were jointly convicted of the gruesome murders of seven young women committed over a period of several years in the sedate city of Gloucester.

This trial followed soon after the conviction of two eleven-year-old boys for the murder of three-year-old James Bulger. About that time there was also a series of racially motivated attacks. Altogether, these crimes had the British public wondering what had happened to a society described by sociologist Geoffrey Gorer in the 1950s as "among the most peaceful, courteous and orderly population the world has ever seen."

It was not just the British people that were shaken. The violence witnessed at soccer games and

111

the riots in sections of Britain's larger cities had many foreigners, especially Americans, wondering what had happened to the country known as the bastion of civilization and refinement.

All this was evidence of a spiralling, apparently out of control, annual rise in crime of around 5%, peaking at 5.7 million offenses in 1992-93.

In 1991, recorded crime rose by 18% in England and Wales. New statistics issued in 1994 indicate a 5% drop in 1994 and a 1% drop in 1993 - the largest fall over a two-year period in about forty years. Police forces at the same time have been reporting sharp falls in offenses, particularly burglary and car crimes.

Much of the improvement in these statistics has been attributed to a change in police policy. They now concentrate on targeting the relatively small number of criminals carrying out the majority of burglaries. In addition, a change of emphasis in government prison policy is based on the simple premise that if persistent criminals are behind bars, they cannot be committing further offenses.

Additional progress has been made as a result of DNA evidence. A national DNA database is building up a genetic profile of prisoners, enabling them to be identified from any traces of blood found at a crime scene.

Another tool being used increasingly in the battle against crime is the use of closed-circuit television monitors, particularly in crime-ridden inner city areas. Downtown Newcastle-upon-Tyne, for example, has seen the number of violent assaults reduced by 19% and criminal damage by 47%.

Do people find these cameras intrusive? Not so, say the police - it is only the criminals who fear the cameras.

Violent crime accounts for just 6% of all recorded crimes committed in Britain. Most of these crimes take place in the home. Unlike the United States, Britain has no written bill of rights, and consequently the public's right to bear firearms is not enshrined by law.

Only a tiny percentage of Brits own guns, and those who do have to go through a fairly rigorous examination before permission is granted. The new Labour Government has promised to outlaw all handguns following the massacre of schoolchildren and their teacher in Dunblane, Scotland.

A large percentage of violent crimes involve the use of knives. The police do not bear arms, except in certain specific situations (see below). The traditional police truncheon, designed years ago, is due to be replaced, but by a more effective truncheon, not by firearms.

The biggest danger to visiting tourists is mugging and personal theft. The chances of this happening are extremely remote, especially if common sense precautions are taken. Keep your money out of sight, keep your diamond-studded tiara tucked away in the hotel safe (why bring it at all?) and don't go walking alone through inner city suburbs late at night.

By and large the Brits are a gentle, peace-loving, non-violent people and you will most likely encounter nothing but warmth and friendship.

Our Police Are Armless

Britain's bobbies - also known as "coppers" - will be a familiar sight throughout your visit. They still wear their dark blue uniforms, but the famous police helmet, worn by bobbies since first introduced in 1863, is going the way of the dodo. It had been as much a British institution as the red telephone box.

However, officers canvassed in a nationwide survey in 1995 claimed that the helmet was uncomfortable, impractical and too conspicuous. When wearing the traditional headgear, officers claimed that villains could "see them coming a mile away." Chasing criminals was a nightmare because the helmet "falls off as soon as we start running." The old-style helmet was an irresistible target for catapult-armed hooligans as well as far too big to wear in a patrol car. It caused police officers to overheat in the hot weather. The traditional helmets, first introduced in 1863, will continue to be worn on ceremonial occasions.

British constables patrol the streets on foot, on bicycles or in cars, giving advice (Canadian and American tourists find them very helpful in giving directions) and dealing with disturbances. They are based at local police stations, where they handle enquiries from the public and deal with arrested people. Some specialize in particular fields, for example, as dog handlers, or as mounted police, and each one of Britain's fifty-two police forces, including the Transport police, has its own criminal investigation department staffed by specialist detectives. Traffic divisions operate road patrol units to enforce the Highway Code and help motorists in difficulties.

There are around 160,000 police officers in Britain. This number will increase substantially by the end of the millennium. In addition, each force has an attachment of volunteer "special constables" who perform certain police duties in their spare time, without pay.

To join the police in England and Wales, you must be at least 18½ years old, be a British or Commonwealth citizen, be physically fit, have good eyesight and pass an aptitude test, regardless of previous academic achievement. The basic training course lasts several months, and is followed by two years service as a "probationer," combining on-the-job training with work at residential centres.

The use of firearms by police has long been a subject of debate in Britain. Only specially-trained officers may carry firearms, and then only on the authority of a senior officer. Such authorization is normally only given when the officer is likely to encounter an armed criminal or when he or she is deployed to protect a person who may be at risk of attack.

Weapons may only be fired as a last resort when officers believe their own or others lives are in danger. Any decision to fire may require justification in court.

Police officers in England and Wales have general powers to "stop and search" if they have reasonable grounds to believe a person is carrying stolen goods, offensive weapons or implements that could be used for theft, burglary or other offenses. In each case, the law requires the officer state and record the grounds for this suspicion, and what, if anything, was found. This "stop and search" policy is unpopular with members of some of Britain's ethnic communities. They claim that they are frequently harassed without justification.

Each police force in England and Wales is responsible to a police authority consisting of local elected councillors (two thirds of the members) and magistrates. In Scotland, the members are directly elected. London's famous Metropolitan Police Force is answerable to the Home Secretary.

Provincial forces are headed by a Chief Constable, Deputy Chief Constable and Assistant Chief Constable. In London, the superior is known as the Commissioner, with a deputy commissioner, deputy assistant commissioner and commander to back him or her up. Other ranks are the same in all forces: chief superintendent, superintendent, chief inspector, inspector, sergeant and constable.

The police authorities appoint the chief, deputy chief and assistant chief constables with the approval of the Home Secretary (or Secretary of State for Scotland). Although the chief constable is responsible for the day-to-day running of the force, he or she is responsible to the police authority for the force's competence, efficiency and conduct.

As opposed to the United States, where the Federal Bureau of Investigation looks into crimes committed against federal law and state or local police investigate crimes against the laws of individual states, Britain has only one layer of criminal law and no equivalent of the F.B.I., although there is talk of establishing a national force.

Some police services are provided centrally, either by government or by co-operation between local forces. In England and Wales, this includes criminal intelligence gathering, telecommunications and research and development.

The National Criminal Intelligence Office provides police forces with information about major criminals and serious crime. Its drugs division co-ordinates drugs intelligence nationally and internationally and helps to coordinate a police and customs response to drug-trafficking.

An independent Forensic Science Service provides aid to police forces in the investigation of crime, working through six regional laboratories and a central research and support establishment. Services are also available to the prosecution and defence in criminal cases.

The Fraud Squad, run jointly by the Metropolitan and City of London Police Forces, provides information to investigators of company fraud in England and Wales.

The National Identification Bureau, run by the Metropolitan Police keeps a record of criminals, their fingerprints and convictions record. It is supported financially by all the police forces.

Regional crime squads are specifically geared to provide an effective response to professional criminals whose activities go beyond an individual force's area of jurisdiction.

Surveys of the British public have shown that the British police are among the most trusted in the world. A recent decline in public confidence came as the result of several high-profile cases where miscarriages of justice were discovered. Restoring public trust in the police is high on the list of government priorities.

A more open approach is being encouraged. This includes publication of information about standards and reorganizing forces along more localized lines. A return to the familiar and comforting sight of the "bobby on the beat" is reassuring to all but criminals.

Police and liaison committees made up of representatives from the police, local councils and community groups operate in every police jurisdiction. Police officers are a familiar sight in schools where they are trying to develop good relations with young people.

Relations between the police and many of Britain's ethnic minorities took a downturn in the 1980s following a series of inner city riots and confrontations. Trainee police officers now receive a thorough training in community relations. Attempts are being made to recruit more members of ethnic minorities to serve in the police force. In 1990, fewer than 2,000 police officers out of a total of 150,000 were members of ethnic minorities.

Arrest and Detention

A statutory code of practice regulates detention, treatment and questioning of suspects by the police. Failure to adhere to its provisions may result in disciplinary proceedings against an officer. Evidence obtained in breach of this code may be ruled inadmissible in court.

A person who has been arrested has a right to contact a solicitor (lawyer) and to ask the police to notify a relative or some other person with an interest in his or her welfare. The police may delay the exercise of these rights for up to thirty-six hours - provided certain strict criteria are met - when a person has been arrested in connection with a serious arrestable offense but has not yet been charged,.

Before any questions are put to a suspect with the purpose of obtaining evidence, that suspect must be cautioned. A controversial change in the law in 1995 decreed that a person's silence could be interpreted as collaboration. For minor offenses, a suspect cannot be held in custody for more than 24 hours. For more serious offenses, the limit is 96 hours. A warrant must be obtained from a magistrates' court after 36 hours. Tape recordings of interviews with suspected offenders is regarded as normal today.

Once there is enough evidence to prosecute a detainee, the police have to decide whether he or she should be charged with the offense. If there is insufficient evidence, the suspect may be released on bail, pending further inquiries. Alternatively, the police may take no further action and release the person, possibly with a caution.

If a person is charged, he may be held in custody only if there is a perceived risk that he might fail to appear in court or interfere in some way with the administration of justice. When no such considerations apply, the person may be released on or without bail. When a person is detained after being charged, he or she must be brought before a magistrates' court quickly, usually no later than the next working day.

The Courts

Many American readers will be familiar with some aspects of British courtroom procedure from watching John Mortimer's "Rumpole of the Bailey" on Masterpiece Theatre or the Poirot and Sherlock Holmes Mystery series on PBS or A&E - or from actually reading Christie, Conan Doyle or P.D. James.

The image of nonagenarian Eton-educated judges in crimson gowns wearing silly wigs dozing their way through hours of testimony is an amusing, but unfair and inaccurate one.

In criminal trials both in England, Wales, and in Scotland, (which has its own legal system) the accused is presumed innocent until proven guilty. Trials take place in open court and the accused is represented by a lawyer. (Trials are never televised - Brits find the thought of television cameras in court quite repugnant) The "Crown Prosecution Service" headed by the government-appointed "Director of Public Prosecutions" is responsible for almost all criminal cases resulting from police investigations.

The most serious cases, such as murder, rape or armed robbery, are tried on indictment by only one of the 90 Crown Courts. All contested trials are presided over by either a High Court judge or a full-time circuit judge sitting with a jury.

Less serious cases - the vast majority - are dealt with by unpaid lay magistrates or by a few stipendiary magistrates, without a jury.

The near 30,000 lay magistrates must be trained in court procedures and be aware of the rules of evidence. They must be recommended for the job by local people through a local committee. The committee tries to ensure that the composition of the bench is balanced. During the proceedings, the lay magistrates are advised on points of law by a justices' assistant or clerk. These courts are normally open to the public and to the media.

Cases involving young people under 18 are usually held in youth courts - specialist magistrates' courts held separately from the mainstream cases.

A third category of offenses known as "either or" cases can be tried *either* by magistrates *or* in a Crown Court.

Just as in the United States and Canada, criminal trials in Britain have two parties: the prosecution and the defence. The prosecution must prove *beyond reasonable doubt* the defendant has committed the crime alleged. In crown court cases, the prosecution must disclose all statements from the witnesses upon whom it proposes to rely.

Rules of evidence are rigorously applied. If evidence is improperly submitted, a conviction may be quashed on appeal.

Crown court trials begin with the reading out of the Indictment, setting out the accusation being made against the defendant. The prosecution then makes its case, backed up by witnesses.

The defendant can address the Court personally or through a lawyer. The lawyer or defendant cross-examines the prosecution witnesses and presents the defence's case backed up by defence witnesses. The prosecution may cross-examine the defence witnesses.

After all the witnesses have given their evidence, the prosecution lawyer makes a closing speech. The defence has the right to the last speech before the case is closed so it follows with its closing.

The Judge's task is to interpret the law, sum up the evidence for the jury and, after hearing the verdict of "guilty" or "not guilty," discharge the accused or pronounce sentence. The judge must take into account the facts of the offense, the circumstances of the offender and possibly previous convictions or offenses before pronouncing sentence.

If the jury cannot reach a unanimous verdict, the judge may permit it to bring a majority verdict, provided there are no more than two dissenters.

The defendant has the right of appeal if found guilty. If the verdict is "not guilty," the defendant cannot be put on trial again for the same offense.

Jurors must be citizens between 18 and 70 years of age whose names appear on the electoral register. There are certain exceptions, such as clergy.

Names are picked at random. Jurors are independent of the judiciary, and any attempt to influence a member of a jury is itself a criminal offense. Potential jurors are put on a panel before a trial, and individual jurors may be challenged. British juries are *never sequestered.*

Sentences passed on a guilty offender are subject to certain limits laid down by Parliament for various offenses. The severity of the punishment reflects the seriousness of the crime. Fines are the punishment for about 80% of offenders. Other sentences include probation, community service or custody "at Her Majesty's Pleasure."

Occasionally, an offender with no previous conviction may be "conditionally discharged," but liable to punishment if convicted of another offense. Others may be bound over to keep the peace. Police cautions are often meted out to young offenders. The caution is a form of warning, and no court action is taken.

Custodial sentences are normally prescribed only for offenders of serious criminal offenses or where the public needs to be protected from a violent and/or sexual offender. A Crown Court can impose a custodial sentence up to life.

A magistrates' court can only impose a maximum term of six months so an offender found guilty in a magistrates' court may be committed for sentencing to the Crown Court. Sentences of less than two years may be suspended for a period of at least a year and not more than two.

Life imprisonment is mandatory for murder

throughout Britain, and is the maximum penalty for serious offenses like rape, armed robbery and arson.

The death penalty, though still technically on the statute books for certain specific crimes - including treason - has not been used since 1957. Public opinion is divided on the issue, with opinion polls indicating that a majority of the public would welcome its return for crimes like murders by terrorists and the killing of police officers. Parliament has consistently voted against making the death penalty available for these crimes.

There are various categories of prisons depending on the nature of the crime committed. They range from "open" prisons to high-security establishments.

The civil law in England and Wales covers matters relating to the family, property, contracts and torts. It also includes constitutional, administrative, industrial, maritime and ecclesiastical law. Scotland has its own system.

Civil proceedings, as a private matter, can often be abandoned or ended by a settlement between the parties out of court. Actions brought to court are usually tried without a jury. Higher courts deal with the more complicated civil cases. Most judgments are for sums of money. Costs incurred must be paid by the defeated party.

The administration of justice in Britain rests with the Lord Chancellor as head of the judiciary, the

Home Secretary, the Attorney General and the Secretary of State for Scotland. The judiciary is independent, without government control. In fact, the courts of the United Kingdom are the Queen's courts, since the Crown is historically the source of all judicial power.

Judges are appointed from among practising lawyers. Barristers or advocates advise on legal problems and present cases in the lay justices and juries courts. Solicitors undertake legal business for individual and corporate clients and can appear in the lay justices courts.

Any citizen in need of legal advice or representation in court may apply for help with the costs from Legal Aid, a government agency designed to help people with limited financial means.

While in Britain, should you find yourself in a situation that could lead to legal action, contact the American Services section of the U.S. Consulate or Embassy.

Chapter Twelve

RELIGION

"The English are not a very spiritual people, so they invented cricket to give them some idea of eternity."　　　　　　　George Bernard Shaw

Little is known of British history prior to 44 AD when Julius Caesar sent his armies to claim what until then had been a mysterious, windswept isle shrouded in mist off the coast of continental Europe.

All over Britain, relics of the Roman occupation remain, if not in an abundance of artifacts, then at least in the names of towns and villages. *Castra*, the Latin for a military camp, gives the modern English Chester and thus, Winchester, Dorchester, and Chichester.

Christianity set down its first, tentative roots in Britain with the arrival of missionaries from Rome or Gaul in the late second and early third centuries. By the year 314, the Church was sufficiently organized to send bishops to the Synod of Arles.

One of the Celtic Church's leading protagonists was Ninian, the son of a converted chieftain of the Cumbrian Britons. He went to Rome as a youth and was instructed in the Christian faith. After consecration as a bishop in 394, he worked to convert Scotland. Ninian's church at Whithorn, in Scotland, became a centre from which he and his monks went out to convert the neighbouring Britons and Picts. It continued as a place of learning for Welsh and Irish missionaries long after his death around 432 AD.

Another major influence in British Christianity was Columba. He landed on the Isle of Iona in the Inner Hebrides in Scotland in 563. The monastery he founded rapidly became the centre for Celtic Christianity. Missionaries were sent out to Scotland and northern England from there. They established several Christian communities. One of them was Lindisfarne in Northumbria, founded by Aidan in 635. Some of these Christian communities became, in turn, important centres of missionary and academic activity.

The scarcity of Christian remains found in the rich villas of the period indicates Christianity was confined to the poorer people at first. Later, in the fourth century, it spread to the upper classes and the army. Christianity became the official religion of the Roman Empire and, thereby, the part of Britain occupied by the Roman forces. This Celtic Church flourished and retained an identity and spirituality quite distinct from the continental Church of Rome. The coming of the Saxons in the fourth century submerged Celtic culture and with it the Celtic Church in England.

In 597 AD Pope Gregory dispatched

missionaries to England. They were led by Augustine, who became chummy with a local king, Ethelbert, in Canterbury. Because of this friendship, Canterbury rather than London, became Augustine's base. Missionaries were sent into much of southern and eastern England from there.

The Celtic Christians found it hard to approve of the Roman Christianity which Augustine summoned them to adopt. The Synod of Whitby in 664 brought bishops of both the Roman and Celtic traditions together to discuss the direction Christianity in Britain should take. The pro-Rome contingent won the day. The Churches of Scotland and Wales eventually conformed to the Roman usages.

The Anglo-Saxons were great church-builders. Some of their small and simple churches still survive. They were also responsible for the construction of much larger cathedrals at London, Winchester and several other cities. These are now either demolished, or so transformed by subsequent architectural additions as to be unrecognizable from the originals.

The Normans were the next to arrive after William the Conqueror defeated the Saxon King Harold at the Battle of Hastings in 1066. Huge, solid, round-arched churches, cathedrals and abbeys were completed during the Norman period. Examples are Westminster Abbey and Durham Cathedral.

Monasticism thrived and many of the monasteries became prosperous. Under the Norman particularly Henry II, a common-law system came into being. For the first time, clergy could be punished for involvement in secular matters. Thomas à Becket, Archbishop of Canterbury, a fierce and outspoken opponent of this law, was murdered in Canterbury Cathedral in 1170 by order from the King.

During the next years, Europe entered the Crusades period, when thousands of knights were packed off to the Holy Land to defend the Christian holy sites against the "infidel" Turks. Richard, the Lion Heart was king but he spent most of his reign away from the country on crusade.

Richard was succeeded by his brother, John. He was noted for his corruption to the point where his barons were ready to overthrow him. However, intervention by the Pope and concessions by the King in the form of the *Magna Carta*, proved sufficient to dissuade them.

John's son, Henry III took over when feudal England was undergoing much upheaval. The Church began to exercise considerable control over secular and political matters as the power of the King as absolute monarch began to diminish. Priests and Bishops took over important political offices such as Chancellor. The Church became wealthier and more corrupt.

By the time Edward I came to the throne, England was a reformed nation with considerable cohesion between Church and State. His son, the bungling Edward II lost Scotland at the Battle of Bannockburn in 1314.

His son, Edward III was notable for restraining the power of the barons. Upon his death in 1377, he was succeeded by his young grandson, Richard II.

However, Henry, Duke of Lancaster had his eyes on the throne. After years of plotting and counter plotting, he proclaimed himself King in 1399. After securing the throne, he had Richard killed. From then until Tudor times, beginning in 1485, England was immersed in serious political and religious intrigue.

On mainland Europe, the arrival of the printing press and the mass-publication of the Bible was having a considerable effect on the population's perception of the Church. In 1517, Martin Luther's blunt challenge to the Roman Catholic Church was the catalyst for a series of changes that swept the continent and had great, though delayed, effects in Britain also.

Henry VIII had good relations with Rome at the start of his reign. As time went on, he needed money to fund his royal wars and campaigns and the Church had plenty. Henry saw a rival and a threat in Cardinal Wolsey, who lived in unashamed luxury at Hampton Court Palace.

At the same time, Henry was desperate for a male heir. His first wife, Catherine of Aragon, bore him a daughter and after several miscarriages and advancing age it became apparent she would not have more children. Henry started looking elsewhere for pleasure as well as political necessity. He did not look far. One of Catherine's ladies in waiting, Anne Boleyn, became the target of Henry's affections. She offered no resistance.

Henry asked the Pope to grant him a divorce. It might have been forthcoming if the Pope had not been surrounded by an army led by Catherine's cousin! Henry thereby passed a series of anti-Church acts. He appointed a lawyer, Thomas Cranmer, to the senior church post in England - Archbishop of Canterbury. Cranmer annulled the merry monarch's marriage to Catherine and he immediately married Anne. In a few months, Anne gave birth - to a girl!

The Pope overruled Cranmer and excommunicated both him and Henry. Cranmer was promoted to the Privy Council. Thomas More, the Chancellor of England, objected to Henry's behaviour and was decapitated. Henry declared himself Supreme Head of the Church of England.

A couple of years later, Henry decapitated Anne and married Jane Seymour. She bore him a son, then died in childbirth.

In effect, what Henry had done was to separate the Church in England from any connection with Rome. "The Bishop of Rome hath no jurisdiction in this realm of England, " the 1549 Prayer Book states. But had Henry intended to create a different Church?

It was mere coincidence that Henry's brush

with Rome came at the same time as earth-shattering religious developments in Germany and other parts of continental Europe. Rampant Protestantism was replacing just about every vestige of the old Church.

In Scotland, the reforming zeal of people like John Knox was stirring up bitter hatred against the Roman Church. His animosity resulted in the abdication of Mary, Queen of Scots in 1567. Protestantism became the official religion of Scotland and Catholicism was suppressed.

Many people in England saw the developments in continental Europe as an opportunity for a new start, a chance to build a new, bible-based, non-sacramental Church. Others, (probably including Henry) had no such desire. The Church might be in need of reform but the sacraments were fundamental to English Church life. Some were prepared to die rather than see the end of English Catholicism.

The result was something of a compromise. A Prayer Book was devised and written by Cranmer. The book contained the essential elements of Catholicism, yet with a more biblically-inspired base.

The religious debate continued after Henry's death and into the reign of his sickly young son Edward VI. Edward's mainly Protestant courtiers were the real power during this period. They oversaw the publication of a new prayer book, the *Book of Common Prayer* to replace the Roman missal. Many of Rome's rituals and ceremonies were in the Book.

In fact, fundamental Protestants described the Book as too Popish.

Edward was succeeded by Mary, Catherine of Aragon's daughter. She had remained a staunch Roman Catholic. Throughout her short reign, she undid much of the work her father had done. She reinstated loyalist Bishops and re-instigated links with Rome. Many non-Catholics, including Cranmer, were burnt at the stake during this period. They became known as the Protestant martyrs.

Mary was childless. When she died, Elizabeth, Anne Boleyn's daughter, acquired the throne. Elizabeth ruled for 45 years, genuinely trying to create a more tolerant atmosphere. The *Elizabethan Settlement* brought about a new understanding of the Church of England as a Church both catholic and protestant. Even so, there were critics. The Protestant wing, especially, castigated the Church of England for its popish rituals and ceremony.

In Scotland, (1560) the reformed Church of Scotland, known as the Kirk, was established on Presbyterian lines. It had its own Confession of Faith and a Book of Discipline.

With the unification of the Scottish and English crowns in 1607, the Stuart kings attempted to make the Kirk episcopal once more. For some decades the pro-episcopal policy prevailed, Episcopacy was established by the Scottish Parliament in 1612. The imposition of the English Prayer Book brought matters to a head in 1637. The following year, the pro-Presbyterian National Covenant was subscribed and the Glasgow General Assembly swept Episcopacy away.

In England, King Charles I supported a more catholic interpretation of the Elizabethan Settlement. Protestants (now known in England as Puritans) were hassled and even killed. Many of them left Britain to form communities in what is now the United States.

The majority stayed on to fight Charles and his High Church Archbishop of Canterbury, William Laud. A seven-year Civil War ensued. Charles I and Archbishop Laud were beheaded. Britain became a republic under the guidance of Oliver Cromwell. During the eleven years period of the Commonwealth, dancing and all forms of public entertainment were outlawed, and the arts were suppressed.

Cromwell died leaving the country in the hands of his weak son, Richard. Charles I's son - also Charles - saw this as an opportunity to reclaim the throne. The *Glorious Revolution* in 1660 saw the re-establishment of the monarchy and the return of Episcopacy in Scotland.

The Great Fire of London of 1666 gave the King an opportunity to rebuild many of the churches. One of them is St. Paul's Cathedral, designed by Sir Christopher Wren. It was finished in 1710, replacing an older, larger building.

When Charles died, his brother James, a devout

Roman Catholic, inherited the throne, and England was again plunged into religious turmoil. In 1688, James II was deposed in a bloodless revolution known as the "Glorious Revolution," for that reason.

He was replaced by Charles II's cousin, William and his wife Mary (II). They were both profoundly Protestant.

After years of bitterness, and even bloodshed, between Scottish Presbyterians and Episcopalians the Church of Scotland became Presbyterian once more (1690) and has remained so ever since. The Scottish Presbyterian Church retains its status as the state Church in Scotland. The unrelated Church of England is the established Church south of the border with the monarch as its supreme governor.

Although the ensuing years were generally peaceful there was still much discontent though the basic structures of British society (and of the established Church) remained relatively intact.

Changes took place between 1740 and 1780 with two revolutions - the Agrarian and Industrial. They brought massive social upheaval. A burgeoning of the building, manufacturing and farming industries, was spurred on by new discoveries and inventions, such as the steam engine.

With its emphasis on thrift and hard work, the Protestant work ethic meant the vast majority of the male population, including children, laboured extremely long hours under exceptionally poor working conditions in the factories and on the farms. Meanwhile, the rich continued to live the life of privilege as was their custom.

The Church of England did little to stand up for the rights of the poor or even to provide them with any spiritual solace. Indeed, they were virtually ignored.

One of the Church of England's clergy, John Wesley, saw the need to take the Christian message out to all the people. His ministry irritated and embarrassed the powers in the Established Church. He travelled thousands of miles on horseback, teaching and preaching to thousands all over the country. He wrote stirring hymns to help get the message across.

As it grew stronger, the Methodist movement angered the Establishment. The Methodists advocated the colonists' cause during the American revolutionary period and stood up for workers' rights at home.

During this period, bloody revolutions broke out in France, resulting in the King and aristocracy being ousted. Many historians contend it was John Wesley and the rise of Methodism that forestalled another bloody revolution in Britain.

Methodism was undoubtedly one of the driving forces behind the general discontent among the masses which prompted the Great Reform Act of 1832. By this act, voting rights were extended to many more people than had previously been eligible.

Queen Victoria's sixty-year reign, which began in 1837, saw increasing political and economic stability and a growing Empire, a genuine desire in many members of the Church of England for social reform and a concern that the Christian message should be taken out to the new colonies.

On the High Church wing of the Church, the Oxford Movement took a highly sacramental brand of Anglicanism to many of the poorest urban areas. Leaders like John Henry Newman and John Keble helped develop far-reaching ministries.

The Evangelical revival was a parallel movement within the Low Church wing of the Church of England and produced similar results. Together, they changed the face of the Church of England. Despite differences that sometimes brought them to blows, they provided hope for many people and helped perpetuate the dual ethos of the Church of England as being both catholic and protestant.

This was also a phenomenal era in Church-building. The majority of Britain's urban churches were built from 1850 - 1900 parallelling the enormous growth in population during this period.

This was also a period of increasing religious toleration; Jews, Dissenters (Nonconformists), atheists and agnostics who had hitherto been excluded from the universities and from positions of authority in public life were now welcomed. Anti-Catholic laws were repealed in the Catholic Emancipation Act of 1829.

Today

By 1990 the number of the British population regularly attending Christian worship had dropped to around ten percent. Total Church membership was around 6.5 million. Membership of the Church of England stood at about 1.9 million, with just under one million attending services regularly - though more than 25 million had been baptized in the Church of England.

Membership of the Roman Catholic Church, hovered around the 2 million mark. Christian denominations total more than 200, and nearly 300 new churches open every year.

Active membership of non-Christian faiths, including Islam, Hinduism and Buddhism has more than doubled in the past twenty years. Prince Charles has spoken openly about becoming "Defender of the faiths" rather than simply "Defender of the faith" when he succeeds to the throne.

Exactly what can the decline be attributed to? Opinion is divided, but many agree the breakdown of the extended family, increasing mobility and general disillusionment, particularly with the Established Church, have been partly responsible. In a 1994 survey, more than half of those interviewed said they believed in God and life after death. Well over half also commented that they felt the Church was out of touch with their daily lives.

The structure of the Established Church has changed little over the past 300 years. The nation is divided into dioceses, each with a Bishop, often an Assistant Bishop or Bishops. Some of them still live in the medieval palaces dating from the days when prelates wielded far more political power than today. Each diocese in turn is divided into geographical parishes, under the leadership of a priest, usually called vicar or rector.

The Church of England is one of Britain's greatest landowners. Much of the revenue is devoured by the cost of maintaining over 18,000 ecclesiastical buildings, many very old and in a poor state of repair.

Although the Church of England is not funded by the state, it is ultimately responsible to Parliament, and cannot legislate without Parliament's approval.

Bishops are appointed by the Queen from nominations presented by the Prime Minister who, in turn, has received a short list of two names from a nominating committee set up by the Church itself. In theory, an atheist or non-Christian Prime Minister can thus pick a Bishop for the Church of England. A number of Bishops sit in the House of Lords.

Most towns have several Anglican parishes, sometimes arranged in teams of three or four churches under the directorship of one Team Rector. Many country clergy have to look after four, five or even more churches.

Because the Church of England is the established church of the land, its clergy are licensed by the state to conduct baptisms, marriages and funerals. Marriages in other denominations must be attended by a representative of the state or be preceded by a ceremony at a register office.

Today, for the vast majority of the population who would describe their religious affiliation as Church of England, these rites of passage are frequently the only real contact they have with their local Church.

Most recently, the mainstream denominations have been working together in ways that would have seemed unthinkable a hundred, even fifty, years ago, with serious dialogue between the Church of England and the Roman Catholic Church in particular. However, the recent vote by the General Synod (the governing body of the Church of England) to allow women to become priests has angered the conservative Roman Catholic leadership and effectively put a hold on further progress.

The battle for the heart and soul of the Church of England moved into a new phase in the 1990s with the issue of women's ordination at the forefront. A new Archbishop of Canterbury, a firm believer in the ordination of women to the priesthood, is perhaps more aware of the inadequacies of the Church than some of his predecessors. He is doing his best to bring about the structural changes that are necessary to ensure the Church remains relevant to people individually and to society at large into the twenty-first century.

Many of the other mainstream churches are experiencing dwindling numbers similar to those of the Church of England. Meanwhile, some of the "house" churches, and the Pentecostal churches have been experiencing significant growth.

In the United States, denominational loyalty is traversed and it is fashionable to shop around for a church. In Britain if you are born Church of England, the chances are you'll die Church of England - even if you never attended a Service in your life.

Church Buildings

Whether you're visiting a tiny twelfth-century village Church or one of the great cathedrals or abbeys, you're likely to be deeply moved. Britain's cathedrals, abbeys, and parish churches are a wealth of architectural styles; treasure-houses of local and national history; and witnesses to the faith of the many generations that built and worshipped in them.

The larger churches are generally open during the daytime. Visitors are welcome to walk around, provided they keep to the permitted areas and obey the rules. Some cathedrals and other large churches charge nominal admission fees, despite howls of protest from the public. They conveniently forget each building costs thousands of dollars a year to maintain and gets only limited assistance from the government.

Visitors who arrive for a look around and are disappointed to find a sign at the door which says, "Service in progress" are welcome to attend the Service (provided, of course, that it is not a private ceremony).

Even if you belong to another religious tradition, attending a Service is a unique opportunity to savor and experience the atmosphere of one of the world's great religious buildings. Plus, you may have the opportunity to hear one of the world's finest choirs, for free!

Many urban churches now close their doors during the week. Rural church buildings are often kept open. They offer a different, yet equally moving experience, reflecting the history of the community over hundreds of years and providing a tranquillity hard to describe. Many of these churches struggle to survive with tiny congregations.

Participation

Services and activities are posted on the church, synagogue or mosque noticeboard, usually facing the street. For many churches, these speak for themselves. For Church of England Parishes, some explanation may be necessary. *Mass* and *Holy Eucharist* on the noticeboard usually indicates a Church within the Catholic tradition of the Church of

England. When *Morning Service* or *Morning Prayer* is posted it usually means a low church tradition is followed. Often *Parish Communion* or *Family Communion* means something in the middle! I wonder what Henry VIII would make of it all.

If you wish to be absolutely certain of the Parish's tradition, call the Vicarage or Parish Office. Most are listed in the telephone directory.

Religious Fundamentalism

Religious fundamentalism does exist in Britain, but exerts nowhere near the amount of political influence as it does in the United States. Christian fundamentalists make up only a tiny proportion of total church membership. Small pockets of fairly vocal Islamic fundamentalists exist in some of the major cities where there have been tensions, but rarely have these resulted in violence.

Chapter Thirteen

THE ROYALS

"A prince is a gr-reat man in th' ol' counthry,
but he niver is as gr-reat over there as he is here."
Finley Peter Dunne: "Prince Henry's Reception."
Observations by Mr. Dooley (1902)

Visitors to the Tower of London are intrigued by the legend about the colony of ravens residing within its hallowed precincts. According to the tradition, if the ravens ever leave the Tower, the British monarchy will collapse. Wisely, as a matter of routine, all the ravens have their wings clipped. This did not stop one of them from being ravaged by a pit bull terrier in 1995.

Political stability in Britain owes much to a system whose continuity has only seriously been disturbed once (during the Republic period, 1649-1660) in well over a thousand years.

The Queen is not only head of state, but an important focus of national unity. In law she is head of the executive, an integral part of the legislature, head of the judiciary, the chief of the armed forces and the Supreme Governor of the Established Church. During the monarchy's long evolution, the absolute power once vested in the monarch has been reduced. Now the Queen is impartial and acts on the advice of her elected government.

Until comparatively recently, public respect and even adulation for the royal family was unquestionable. A poll conducted before the separation of the Prince and Princess of Wales indicated more than 75% of the great British public wanted to see the monarchy survive.

Today, despite the immense popularity of the Queen Mother, the esteem and respect reserved for Princess Anne, (who has devoted much of her life to charitable work) and affection for the Queen herself, the future of the Windsor dynasty hangs in the balance.

In 1995, in a similar poll, half of those interviewed indicated they did not believe there would be a monarchy within fifty years. Many still regard the monarchy as a sensible and useful institution, not least for the fact it is a focus of national identity "above" party politics. The monarchy provides immunity from the kind of corruption and in-fighting often characteristic of leadership elections elsewhere.

People tolerated this self-perpetuating class system so long as those at the top of the pyramid retained a mystic aura. Some claim it's this sense of "mystery" that enabled the royal family to survive for so long. However, things are changing.

The reasons for the decline in support for Britain's most enduring, if not endearing, institution are legion. For one thing, unlike the half-dozen or so other remaining monarchies in Europe, the British royal family is often seen as being remote and out of touch with ordinary people. 1992 was dubbed an *Annus Horibilis* by Her Majesty, the Queen after a series of family problems. The separation of the heir to the throne and his wife and the burning down of part of Windsor Castle, the Queen's favourite residence were two of them. At the same time, millions of ordinary Brits lost their jobs and homes in a serious recession which gripped the country.

Salt was rubbed into the wound when the Queen asked the country to pay for repairs to the castle. Perhaps not an unreasonable request, except that up until that point, Her Majesty had not been paying taxes. The Queen's offer to pay income taxes in the future, though welcomed, was too late to have had any beneficial effect on public opinion.

Then, as the Government sat down to consider drastic cuts in the nation's defence expenditure, it was heard the worn-out, royal yacht Britannia might be replaced with a newer model at vast public cost.

Some of the Queen's extended family, many of whom received income from the public purse, came under growing public criticism for not giving their money's worth.

But most damaging of all have been the personal problems of the Queen's children. Anne was divorced and has since remarried; Andrew first separated then he and Sarah Ferguson divorced. Most serious was the breakdown of the marriage of Prince Charles, heir to the British throne, and Princess Diana. They engaged in a very public battle for the sympathy of the British people.

Charles' long-time romance with Camilla Parker-Bowles and the broadcasting of the "Camillagate" tapes was exposed. Then the Princess's admitted affair with James Hewitt and her liaison with others was openly discussed. Books, television programs, accusations, counter-accusations and a no-holds-barred conflict - altogether an abandonment of traditional royal reticence.

The royal soap opera came to a head in 1995 with a letter from the Queen to both parties urging them to consider a divorce.

Certain members of the royal family may have acted foolishly, but surely in no more serious a way than countless others have in the past.

Never has a British Royal Family had to contend with such intense scrutiny and relentless publicity as the present generation, especially from the mass-circulation tabloids.

In this Hollywood era, the royals are expected to look like movie stars, dripping with diamonds and studded with pearls. A comment in the sermon given at Charles and Di's 1981 wedding by the then Archbishop of Canterbury, Robert Runcie, "This is the stuff of which fairy tales are made." served to perpetuate this fairy-tale, Brothers Grimm image.

Yet they are expected to behave quite differently from movie stars. High ethical standards are expected - to the point of sainthood. For every lapse, even momentary, somebody is watching - usually with a camera. Servants who once had sworn fealty, are ready to spill the beans - for a price. The tabloid newspapers, those self-appointed guardians of the public good are anxious to snap up any snippet of royal gossip. They must surely spend a fortune in long-lens cameras.

An Edwardian lady, Mrs. Patrick Campbell, once said, "It doesn't matter what you do in the bedroom, as long as you don't do it in the streets and frighten the horses."

Lord McGregor, chairman of the Press Complaints Authority from 1991-1994 has commented, "The media frenzy has had the effect of shifting the bedrooms of some of the young royals onto the streets."

Words are distorted. A man in a crowd shouted out, "You've lost a good woman there, sir" to the Prince of Wales. After the Prince smiled at the man, apparently in agreement, the headline in the following morning's papers ran, "Prince admits to losing a good woman."

Even the BBC, which once automatically offered its unswerving devotion to the royal family like some loyal lady-in-waiting, has become more objective in its reporting of royal matters. Gone is the bowing and scraping that once characterized the relationship. The overall result of all this, some say, will be to destroy the institution of the monarchy.

Sections of the press have been uncompromising in their determination to not only wash the royal family's dirty linen in public, but to rake up as much muck as it can. On one occasion, the *Sun* sarcastically invited its readers to fax their messages of goodwill to Princess Anne on the occasion of her second marriage. Despite an estimated readership of more than twelve million, not one message was received, announced the paper, smugly.

The fact that virtually no Sun reader possesses a fax machine is beside the point. The episode illustrates very clearly the hostility between the Palace and the popular press - and the depths to which some newspapers will sink to trash the royals and boost circulation. Indeed the only beneficiaries from the House of Windsor's current woes are the royal biographers (still Britain's leading growth industry) and the powerful media barons.

With no bill of rights to protect the privacy of the individual and a toothless Press Complaints Commission whose only action has been to say it is "distressed" by the behaviour of certain sections of the press, maybe it's time for a new *Magna Carta*.

Meanwhile, the poor old Queen has to raise money somehow to pay her bills. A few years ago,

Buckingham Palace opened its doors (some of them) to the lower orders of the British public and American tourists at $12 a throw. Even then, the cynical press was quick to find fault. They pointed out - with some degree of satisfaction - that on the first day of opening only 4,300 tickets were sold, far fewer than the 7,000 expected.

While many of the public were impressed, not surprisingly, many of the media were not. Lloyd Grossman, an American journalist working in Britain, described the state rooms as, "a mixture between a curry-house and an over-the-top Hollywood set from the 1920s." Hollywood sets are so accurate! He went on to say he found plastic flower pots, "linoleum masquerading as marble," threadbare carpets, no books anywhere and magnificent fireplaces spoiled by two-bar electric fires everywhere. Sounds just like any typical British home.

Another correspondent, this time for London's *Independent* newspaper, likened the Palace to a "Down-at-the-heel railway hotel in a provincial city, revamped perhaps in the 1950s and 60s."

The *Telegraph's* critic waxed lyrical about the wall coverings and the crystal chandeliers, but went on to describe it as "Hideous beyond my powers of description; a cacophonous jungle of screaming crimsons, golds, and Prussian blues, a jumble of furniture from every century and style thrown together in the hope they will cancel each other out."

The Palace rooms will remain on view for five years. The fees are expected to raise $6 million or so towards the $40 million cost of repairing Windsor Castle.

Up until now, the royal family has been synonymous with the nation. While Americans sing *God Bless America*, Brits croon, *God Save the Queen*. Reverence for the monarch is Britain's way of patting itself on the back - an ancient self-esteem mechanism which has served the nation well for centuries.

The country has been desperately trying to come to terms with the loss of its vast Empire and in recent years the demise of its manufacturing base. The government's proposal, in the early 1990s, to close the coal mines was a massive psychological blow to the nation which gave birth to the coal-based Industrial Revolution. The people have also witnessed a continuing movement towards European unity. The Monarchy's brand of staid, solid respectability may seem a little dull, but it has had a powerful, moderating, pacifying effect.

The future for the British family may be uncertain, but not totally hopeless. The Queen, who has worked unstintingly for the good of the nation continues to command tremendous respect, not only in Britain, but throughout the Commonwealth and wider world.

I have no doubt a trimmer monarchy will come

out of this present situation, but I'd still be making sure those ravens are firmly chained to their perches. Just in case...

Chapter Fourteen

POLITICS

"Political skill is the ability to foretell what is going to happen tomorrow, next week, next month, next year. And to have the ability to explain afterwards why it didn't happen."

Sir Winston Churchill

For most North American visitors, trying to understand British politics is as difficult as filling in your IRS tax returns. Although both American and Canadian systems have their roots in the British political system, there are some significant differences.

The United Kingdom of Great Britain and Northern Ireland is a parliamentary democracy comprising England, Scotland, Wales and Northern Ireland. It is a constitutional monarchy (although there is no written constitution, or bill of rights). The Head of State and Commander-in-Chief of the armed forces is the Sovereign.

The monarch has no direct political power for various historical reasons. However, she or he does have *theoretical power*. The monarch can make peace or war, issue charters, create peers, summon and dissolve Parliament. In reality, it would be unthinkable for the Sovereign to act against the

155

wishes or the advice of the elected Government. This is deliberate.

Britain's history is littered with kings and queens who have claimed to act by divine right. The English Civil War, which concluded dramatically with the reduction of the 4' 6" tall King Charles I into a beheaded four-foot King Charles I, effectively put an end to such autocracy.

Today, the monarch is very much the symbol of the nation - a rallying point and a focus. When you see vans marked Royal Mail, do not assume this is the Queen's own personal postal service. In British courtrooms, a case against a defendant is still introduced as "Her Majesty versus . . ." Official government correspondence, including tax returns, are marked "On Her Majesty's Service."

Britain is, in practice, governed by Parliament. The two Houses of Parliament, Commons and Lords, meet in the Palace of Westminster. The lower (and more important) of the two Houses is the House of Commons. Viewers of C-SPAN see the - apparently - vicious slanging matches that rage across the floor of its hallowed precincts, especially during Prime Minister's Question Time. (They all love each other really).

The nation is divided into nearly 700 constituencies, each of which votes for its own Member of Parliament (MP) to sit in the Commons. The political party with the largest number of MPS usually forms the Government.

Voting is by universal suffrage - every British citizen aged eighteen and over is entitled to participate in national and local elections. A General Election must be held at least every five years, but this period may be much shorter. The party in government has the right to call an election at any time, provided it gives proper notice to the opposing parties. This is particularly useful to them if their majority is small, and they are riding high in the opinion polls.

The run-up to an election is an exciting time, partly because it only lasts for a few months and is not as exacting or time-consuming as the race for the U.S. presidency. (The U.S. election date is fixed, and the campaigning starts a year or more in advance.)

A by-election is held if an MP resigns or dies during his or her term of office.

At election time, a humorous dimension is added to the serious political debate by the presence in some constituencies of bizarre and frequently eccentric contestants. Screaming Lord Sutch's "Monster Raving Loony Party" is by far the most famous. With a deposit of just £500, any British citizen of age can contest a constituency at an election. The deposit is forfeited if they fail to win at least 5% of the total votes cast.

Unlike the American system, voters do not register their party political affiliation prior to the election. In Britain's "first past the post" electoral system, the candidate with the highest number of votes (it need only be a majority of one) is declared the winner.

Once elected, an MP casts votes on important national and international issues and represents the interests of his or her constituency in the Chamber of the House of Commons. Debates on controversial topics such as when a whiff of scandal is in the air or where the government is on the ropes for some U-turn on policy draw a capacity crowd of MPs.

In such cases, government and opposition whips encourage all members of the party to be present. A free vote takes place when there is no official party line on an issue. Members need not vote along party lines.

The raucous, frenzied scenes so often shown on television usually take place during the Prime Minister's Question Time. This is a period during which the Prime Minister (or, in his absence, another senior minister acting on his behalf) answers questions from the floor of the House.

The layout of the Chamber is modeled on the traditional public school/Oxbridge Chapel and helps to heighten the sense of confrontation. The two major parties face each other, their leaders glaring across the front bench - only a few feet of space separating them.

Presiding over the proceedings is the Speaker

who is expected to be totally impartial in dealing with members of the House, even though he or she is also an elected MP with a duty to represent his or her constituents.

It's a tough task, especially when the government is having a bad day and the opposition is doing its best to exploit the situation. It's even more uncomfortable when you are wearing a wig.

Scenes like this are but a small portion of what goes on in the House most of the time. Usually a handful of MPs debate less contentious issues. Much of an MP's work takes place in committee and in the constituencies. Many of them hold regular "surgeries" for constituents needing help.

Britain's two major political parties are the Conservatives (commonly known as the Tories.) Their emphasis is on free enterprise and private ownership. The other major party is the Labour Party, with its roots in the union movement.

Lately, their political emphases are changing. Labour has turned from its far-left idealism of the 1970s to a more moderate stance on a variety of issues and its new leadership is trying to distance itself from union domination. At the same time, big business, the traditional ally of the Tories, has been steadily deserting that party since the demise of Margaret Thatcher's government.

Members on both sides of the House (but especially vociferous on the Conservative side) are wary of Britain's membership in the European Community. They dread a gradual erosion of sovereignty from their Mother of Parliaments to the European Parliament in Strasbourg, France - to which British voters also elect members. For them, the greatest demon of all is the move towards a single European currency which could eventually mean the abolition of the beloved pound sterling.

A third party, the Liberal Democratic Party is a hybrid of the old Liberal Party of William Ewert Gladstone and the Social Democratic Party (a political phenomenon of the 1970s.)

The Liberal Democrats are hampered by the "first past the post" electoral system. However, the 1997 General Election saw a major breakthrough. Fifty Liberal Democrat MPs were elected - the largest quota for many years.

A further complication is the strong nationalist sentiment in both Scotland and Wales. When you realize the opposition Conservative Party is not represented by any MPs in Scotland, maybe the resurgence of Scottish nationalism is not so surprising.

Today, despite something of a revival in the fortunes of the Scottish Nationalist Party, it has never been able to make a breakthrough. By far the largest party in Scotland is the Labour Party.

The new Labour Government has promised to devolve some of Westminster's legislative powers to a new, elected Scottish Assembly based in Edinburgh. They also promised a Welsh Assembly located in Cardiff.

The head of Government in Britain is the Prime Minister. Unlike the President of the United States, he or she is not elected for the office by the people. The Prime Minister is the leader of whichever party (or coalition of parties) happens to have the largest number of MPs in the House. Tory leaders are normally chosen by a ballot of their MPs. Labour leaders by a vote of all party members nationwide (including unions with block votes).

The Prime Minister presides over a Cabinet of Senior Ministers, each with responsibility for his or her own department, ranging from Foreign Affairs to the Environment. The Opposition mirrors this with its own "shadow cabinet."

The Prime Minister wields authority in a different way. The term *primus inter pares*, frequently used to describe the Prime Minister's status as chairperson of the cabinet, conveniently conceals the more authoritarian, presidential style some Prime Ministers have chosen to employ.

The Prime Minister's official London residence is Number 10 Downing Street in Whitehall. Attempted terrorist attacks in recent years have resulted in the street no longer being accessible to the general public. A large country retreat called Chequers also comes with the job.

The Upper House of Parliament is the House of Lords composed of around 1,200 lords. Included are the twenty-six Lords Spiritual - the Archbishops of Canterbury and York, the Bishops of London, Durham and Winchester and twenty-one other senior bishops of the established Church of England; the Lords Temporal - peers by descent of England, Scotland, Wales or the United Kingdom and new peers, Lords of Appeal and Life Peers (like Baroness Thatcher). Many of the Life Peers are former members of the House of Commons.

The principle underlying the Commons/Lords system is that the Lords, as a revising chamber, should complement the Commons and not rival it.

Occasional televised debates depict sleepy nonagenarians barely able to keep their eyes open. Access is hampered by dozens of walker frames cluttering up the doorway. Veteran Labour MP Tony Benn said (long before he was a veteran), "The British House of Lords is the British Outer Mongolia for retired politicians."

In recent years, talk of reorganization of the House of Lords or even replacing it with an elected assembly has been heard. So far, there has been very little action.

New laws start out as *bills* and can be introduced either by the Government as a whole, or by an individual member (a private member's bill). All bills except money bills, must originate in the

Commons. A bill can be introduced in either House, where it receives its *first reading*. The next stage is the *second reading* when it is debated by the House.

If passed, it is referred to a committee, either a committee of the whole House, a Select Committee (appointed for a specific purpose) or a Standing Committee. This is known as the *Committee Stage*. In the committee stage, the bill is discussed in detail clause by clause until being returned to the House with or without amendment.

The next step is the Report Stage. The bill is either accepted or referred back to the same or another committee.

Eventually, if it survives this far, the bill receives its *Final Reading* and is sent to the other House. Once a bill has been passed by both Houses, and has received the *Royal Assent* it becomes an *Act of Parliament*.

Technically, a sovereign could veto it, but this has not been done since the time of Queen Anne in the early eighteenth century. If exercised, it would precipitate a constitutional crisis. The Queen and her family are expected to be above party politics, and controversy inevitably ensues when a statement made by any one of them is interpreted by the media to be political.

The Queen does not set foot inside the Commons. Each November, in an elaborate ceremony known at the State Opening of Parliament, all MPs

163

are summoned to the Chamber of the House of Lords, where the Lords are already seated in their full regalia, to listen to the Queen's Speech - not a personal speech, but a statement prepared by Her Majesty's Government, outlining their agenda for the coming parliamentary session.

Policies are implemented by government departments and executive agencies staffed by politically neutral civil servants. They serve the government of the day regardless of its political persuasion.

Visitors, including non-British citizens, are permitted to watch debates from public galleries in both Houses. Entry is free. However, you'll have to queue. If the debate taking place is of a controversial nature, the line might be very long indeed.

The Palace of Westminster

This is the official title of the familiar Parliament building, flanked at one end by *St. Stephen's Tower* which houses *Big Ben*. Parliament has been held on this site since 1340. It was then a royal palace.

The original was built by Edward the Confessor and enlarged by William the Conqueror. Over the years, many alterations were made. Then, in 1834, the whole pile was destroyed by fire except for Westminster Hall - dating from the time of William II.

The new building, was built on the same site

between 1840 and 1867 by Sir Charles Barry and Augustus Pugin. Contrary to popular belief, Big Ben is not the name of the 316 foot tower at the building's eastern end which houses the world's most famous clock. Big Ben is the huge 24 cwt bell which chimes the hours. It's named after Sir Benjamin Hall, the first clerk of works of the new building.

The Chamber of the House of Commons was destroyed during a bombing raid in 1941. It was replaced by an almost-but-not-quite identical chamber, used for the first time in 1950.

Local Government

Elected local authorities in Britain range from large metropolitan district councils and county councils to unitary authorities, town and rural district councils.

All exercise powers and duties are given to them by Parliament, including the provision of housing, education, personal social services, police and fire brigades. Their expenses are met partly by grant from central government and partly by a local tax, known as the council tax. Local elected councillors are expected to act on behalf of members of their ward needing help or advice.

Unlike the American system, voters in Britain do not cast ballots for individual officers such as school committee members. Once a local authority has been elected, these posts are apportioned among the elected councillors.

Chapter Fifteen

MONEY

"I'm tired of Love: I'm still more tired of Rhyme./But Money gives me pleasure all the time. "
Hilaire Belloc, *Fatigue*

Money has always been a worry when traveling overseas. You may ask, "Am I taking enough? What if I run out?"

It is less of a problem today. The worldwide use of credit cards and, more recently, the installation of the Cirrus and Yankee 24 systems at cash machines (ATMs) all over the world, means you can obtain cash from your home checking account in local currency twenty-four hours a day. MasterCard, Visa and American Express are widely used in Britain.

Traveler's checks are still useful. If they are lost or stolen, they can be replaced - unlike your cash. It's worth noting that traveler's checks are virtually never used as cash in Britain.

Dollar traveler's checks can normally be purchased at virtually any bank in North America and at some travel agents, such as AAA, American Express and Thomas Cook's.

British pounds traveler's checks are also available, but don't expect your local bank to keep them in stock. Usually they must be ordered unless you're in a large city that has a downtown bank with a foreign currency section.

It is sensible to bring some cash in British pounds to cover incidental expenses immediately after your arrival, such as Underground or taxi fares, tips etc. Larger banks may have pounds in stock, or you may have to wait a week or two while they are being ordered. Another option is to purchase British pounds at the airport before you depart.

In any case, it makes sense to keep an eye on the exchange rates for a couple of months or so before you leave and *during your stay.* Daily exchange rates are published in most national and regional daily newspapers in North America and Britain, in the windows of British banks, *bureaux de change,* certain post offices and in many hotels, especially those frequented by foreign tourists.

The most favorable exchange rates are offered by financial institutions and currency exchange firms (Thomas Cook and American Express have many branches in the UK). Hotels, restaurants and shops are unlikely to give you as good an exchange rate. Make sure you have picture identification. A passport is best because British people are not accustomed to seeing driver's licenses with photographs!

If you're carrying a lot of cash on your person, keep it well hidden. Like all countries, Britain has its fair share of pickpockets and other criminals who'd just love to make off with your money. A large bulge on your right buttock advertises that you have a full wallet and are just dying for someone to steal it. A large handbag (pocketbook) will also be regarded by Mr. Swag as fair game. Britain is generally safe provided you use your common sense.

The currency in Britain is the pound sterling. Once, in the halcyon days prior to World War I, the pound occupied the prestigious position of being the world's leading currency - just as the U.S. dollar does today.

The British pound was divided into twenty shillings, each shilling itself divided into twelve pence (singular: penny). Despite the complications of such an archaic system, the British (who would all surely have qualified for a Master's degree in Arithmetic), reluctantly saw the system replaced by a decimal system in 1971. Many complained it was an indirect way the government used to raise money. Certainly prices did seem to rise at the time but runaway inflation was the main culprit.

In 1971, the 240 pennies of the pre-decimalization pound were replaced by 100 new pennies. Shillings were abolished, although the shilling and two-shilling coins remained in circulation for some time, doubling up as five pence pieces and ten-pence pieces respectively. Twenty-five years on, many older Brits still lament the change, and yearn to return to the days of the "old money." Certainly, the change caused a great deal of confusion, especially among the elderly.

Outrage was added to injury in the 1980s. In England and Wales the much loved green "pound note" was replaced by a pound coin (Scotland chose to retain the note).

Now, the British are on the warpath about the European Community's apparent desire to establish a European currency, probably involving the *abolition* of the British pound - a horror more likely to unite the British people than anything since the Second World War. Whatever next!

Today's coin denominations are:

- The pound (£)
- The fifty-pence piece (a seven sided phenomenon)
- The twenty-pence piece (also seven-sided)
- The ten pence piece (much the same size as a quarter)
- The five-pence piece (the same size as a dime)
- The two-pence piece
- The penny (much like a cent coin in size).

Getting the feel (literally) of a different currency always takes time, especially when you are trying to convert the transaction into dollars at the same time. Eventually, just when you do master it, it will be time to leave!

Sometimes you'll hear the pound referred to by its slang name, "quid." Note that quid never takes a plural s. People talk about twenty quid, fifty quid etc. - not quids.

Paper money (notes) is issued in the following denominations: £50; £20; £10 and £5 plus £1 in

170

Scotland. Unlike U.S. currency which, until recent changes in the size and design of the $100 bill, came in one size and colour, British paper currency comes in different sizes, colours and designs. Scotland has its own notes with different designs. They are also legal tender in England and Wales, just as English cash is legal in Scotland.

Note: One of the surest ways to anger the British on both sides of the border is to offer them a large denomination note for a relatively small purchase (e.g. a £50 for purchase of less than £10 in a pub, or £10 for a sixty pence bus fare). You may have to contend with considerable verbal abuse. The seller will take delight in revenge, such as giving you your change in hundreds of small-denomination coins.

I have also witnessed American tourists offering dollars for purchases made in a store, pub, or restaurant. Nothing, not even burning the Flag or mocking the Royal Family will irritate the normally cool and polite Brits more than this. After all, how would you feel if someone offered you British pounds for a purchase made at home? Such insensitive behaviour does nothing for transatlantic relations.

MasterCard, Visa, American Express and Diner's Club cards are widely accepted in Britain, but not everywhere. Most establishments display the cards they honour in their window. Don't look out for the *name* of the credit card company, look for the

171

symbol. In Britain, MasterCard is usually known as Access and Visa as Barclaycard. Don't be surprised if you are met with a look of total consternation when you ask, "Do you accept MasterCard?" The British are more apt to use checks, (spelt cheques) or cash for their purchases.

You can't use your own U.S. personal checks for purchases made in Britain. Don't automatically assume every restaurant accepts a credit card. If you're going to be in Britain for a long time, you might consider opening a bank account.

Another thing to watch out for is how much it's *really* going to cost you to make a particular purchase. Most purchases made overseas with a U.S. credit card are not processed the day the transaction is made. Therefore, the rate of exchange is unlikely to be calculated on the day you made the purchase. If the dollar does well over the next few days and weeks, all is well. You may pay even less for your purchase than you anticipated. If, however, the dollar is in the doldrums, you may be shocked when your credit card invoice arrives.

London still regards itself as the financial capital of the world - a claim hotly disputed by New York, Tokyo, and even Frankfurt. British Banks have a strong reputation for conservative solidity. This includes the four or five High Street Banks whose branches you'll see in just about every town and city throughout the country.

Around thirty years ago British banks underwent the same process happening in the U.S. today. A plethora of small, often local, institutions were swallowed up by their larger neighbours. The result was four megabanks - Barclay's, Lloyds, Midland and National Westminster - and a dozen or so smaller institutions (Co-op Bank, Royal Bank of Scotland etc.). You are also likely to see their branches from time to time.

Most of Britain's mortgage business is conducted by the myriad *building societies* you'll observe in every High Street. Deregulation of the financial industry in the last decade led to a liberalization of their services. Today, High Street banks vie with building societies for mortgage business and building societies are beginning to offer the more general banking services provided by the banks. Many building societies offer checking and savings accounts, credit cards and ATM cards. So if you're looking for an ATM bear in mind the building society round the corner may also accept your card.

You'll need to find a branch of American Express, Thomas Cook or a bank with a Foreign Exchange Department to change dollars cash or traveler's checks to pounds. These are usually located in the downtown districts of most medium and large size towns and cities. They are open Monday through Friday, 9:30 AM till 3:30 PM. An increasing number are open Saturday mornings and, with deregulation of Sunday trading, on Sundays.

173

If you have used up every penny you have and have reached the credit limit on all your cards, both American Express and Western Union have branches in Britain. Arrangements can be made with them to transfer funds from the U.S. to the U.K. You will, of course, need identification (preferably a passport).

SECTION THREE

ATTRACTIONS

Chapter Sixteen

ACCOMMODATIONS

"All saints can do miracles, but few of them can keep a hotel."   Mark Twain, "Notebook"

A wide choice of accommodations are available for you in Britain. Choose from deluxe hotels, converted stately homes, family run guesthouses, B&B's (Bed & Breakfast), youth hostels and caravan parks (trailer parks). Prices vary according to quality, services provided and location.

In addition to these more conventional forms of accommodations, unusual alternatives abound. You can stay at a farmhouse (not in central London) and share the family life. Interested in history? Stay at a castle.

Self-catering options are plentiful. Rent a seaside holiday flat or a country cottage dripping with sweet-smelling wisteria. Since you do your own housework - or hire it done - and buy your own groceries, this choice generally costs less.

Accommodations in Britain can be expensive, especially in London, Edinburgh and other main visitor destinations. A lot depends on the exchange rate. If the British pound is weak and the dollar is strong *at the time you pay* for your accommodations, they may appear more reasonable.

Hotels range in size from the huge international chain hotels, such as Sheraton and Trusthouse Forte, to tiny and much less expensive family run establishments. The large hotels may have 1,000 rooms or suites - or more. They offer many luxurious and convenient amenities.

You're more likely to meet and get to know the British people at the small hotels. They may have rooms with a bath or you may have to share a bath - often a short jaunt down the hall.

The important thing is . . . do your homework. Find out exactly what is offered, before you make your reservations. Familiarize yourself with the country's hotel classifications systems.

The Crown System, devised by the English, Scottish and Welsh Tourist Boards, classifies all participating hotels into six categories. Five crowns is the highest rating through to one crown.

A further category of hotels are simply "listed." This does not mean they are the dregs. They must be clean and well maintained to make the list at all, but they don't offer as wide a range of services as their multi-crowned counterparts.

Lists of participating hotels are available from the specific tourist authorities or from local tourism offices all over Britain.

This system has been criticized for a variety of

reasons:

- ▸ Establishments request and pay for inspection and rating.
- ▸ Many hotels have not joined the system so if you rely on it, you may not have a complete idea of what is available.
- ▸ The crowns indicate the presence or absence of certain specified facilities but do not testify about the *quality* of the accommodations. Having a bathroom with a solid marble floor and gold faucets will not make up for a leaky loo (toilet) or a telephone that doesn't work.

Britain's two leading motorist associations, the Automobile Association (AA) and the Royal Automobile Club (RAC), operate another classification system. The system uses stars instead of crowns to rate accommodations. They also have an additional category called approved. Copies of the AA and RAC rated places are usually in the glove compartments of cars rented from companies associated with them. You can also purchase their rating list in many bookstores and travel centers.

All hotels participating in both systems must have adequate heating. Many of the highly rated and more expensive hotels also have air-conditioning.

Many British hotels offer breakfast which they include in the price of the room. It is worth it to check this out - you haven't lived until you have sampled the delights of a full English breakfast. A "continental" breakfast pales into insignificance beside it.

Many hotels serve evening meals but they rarely include the price in the room rate.

Make sure you have an idea of what you final charges will be. A 10% or 15% service charge and a 17.5% Value Added Tax (VAT) will be added to your bill. Of course, the domestic staff always appreciates a tip.

Look for inns in many smaller towns and cities, such as Canterbury, Salisbury and York. Some of them have been providing accommodations to travelers for centuries. In many of them original features like hand-hewn ancient beams, huge fireplaces and four-poster beds have been preserved. You will experience a distinctive atmosphere in an ancient inn.

Since most of these inns started as drinking establishments, in many of them the focal point is still the bar. It is usually open to all, whether or not they are guests of the inn.

Despite their venerability, many inns have been modernized and refurbished to high standards. Private bathrooms, television, radio and telephones are often provided. British hotels inevitably have tea and coffee making equipment in each room. There may be an assortment of snacks and drinks (honor system) available also.

Even if you must make a short walk along the

corridor to get to the bathroom, it is a small price to pay for possibly bathing in the same bathtub as Elizabeth I!

Guesthouses are small hotels, often run and lived in by the same family that owns them. There is a preponderance of them at seaside resorts, but they can also be found in other tourist centers. The British "seaside landlady" is a national institution, the butt of a million vaudeville jokes over the years.

When you stay in a guesthouse, you'll often find the sea just a stone's throw away. The shrieking of the seagulls will contrast with the polite, almost whispering breakfast conversation of Brits on holiday. A full English breakfast, lovingly cooked and served, is usually included in the basic price. An evening meal of hearty home cooking may be available at an additional cost.

It is very likely you will share a bathroom but you will probably have your own washbasin with hot and cold running water. The hotel's brochure may proudly boast about this as if it is some kind of special luxury.

Don't expect TV or a telephone in your room but there is almost certain to be a resident's lounge with a television (if you have nothing better to do) and a pay phone may be somewhere on the premises - usually the lobby.

Accommodations at a guesthouse will be

simple, but they will be clean and you will really feel you are in Britain. That fearsome landlady, portrayed in skits as a relentless dragon, will more than likely go out of her way to make you feel at home. She can give you helpful advice and recommendations on places to go and see - and how to get to them.

Note: Small places like guesthouses are highly unlikely to accept credit cards.

Bed and Breakfasts (B&Bs) are private homes with a few, inexpensive rooms for letting. There is usually a prominently displayed sign outside identifying the premises as a B&B and specifying "Vacancy" or "No Vacancy."

You can drive around and look for a sign or if you are less spontaneous, a list of local B&Bs is available at the tourism office. The office can help you with reservations, too.

You'll find yourself in a minority as far as nationality goes. Both guest houses and B&Bs are immensely popular with the thrifty Brits. Some of them have come back to the same establishment for donkey's years and regard it as their second home.

B&Bs are usually not luxurious, but they should be clean and comfortable. You might even strike lucky and find a room with an *en suite* bath.

What you lack in facilities, you'll make up for in the homely ("homely" in Britain is a compliment) atmosphere and your close, friendly encounters with the owner and other residents. You will find great enthusiasm for the locality. The owner will be happy to advise you on places to visit and things to do. You can learn history about local places, families and events never mentioned in a book. The owner will even give you all the gossip about his or her own family!

Breakfasts are home-cooked and often sumptuous. An evening meal may be provided at extra cost. B&Bs seldom accept credit cards.

Stately homes are quite a contrast to B&Bs. These huge homes were once the preserve of aristocrats but now they are often the homes of aging rock stars. Increasingly, sections of them have been converted to provide accommodations for paying visitors. Usually, the homes have successfully retained their historic atmosphere and ambiance. Expect to be impressed by glorious settings in parklands, near rivers or lakeside. History oozes out of ancient fireplaces, antique furnishings and art.

You may be even more impressed by the fact you have your own bathroom, TV and telephone.

Many stately home accommodations maintain exceptionally high standards of cuisine. They use quality fresh ingredients from the local countryside. Indeed, the dining room may be a magnet for local residents from miles around.

Self-catering (rental) accommodations are available in all shapes and sizes throughout Britain. You can rent purpose-built "holiday flats" with all amenities, sea views and those screeching gulls. You can live in an ancient cottage set in magnificent peaceful countryside. Or perhaps your taste runs to downtown city apartments, convenient for pubs and restaurants, historical sights and public transport connections.

Because you have to visit the local food store or supermarket, top up the tank with petrol (gas) or stand in the queue at the bus stop, self-catering your accommodation is a great way to feel you're a real part of the locality. There is another bonus - you are likely to have more space and privacy than you would have in a hotel room.

Self-catering accommodations come in all states of quality form deluxe to simple, no frills. You can expect to find certain necessities in just about all of them - heating, a bathroom with a tub (but not always a shower), a television, a cooker (stove), a fridge (refrigerator), cooking utensils, the inevitable electric kettle, crockery (dishes), silverware and cleaning materials.

The main drawback for many people is that you must do your own housework or have it done at your expense. Of course, you will venture out to buy basics like washing-up liquid, groceries, etc.

Note: In a minority of rentals, daily cleaning service is included.

You will be asked for a deposit and/or required to buy insurance to be sure you hand back the property in the same clean and tidy state in which you should have found it.

Brochures for self-catering accommodations will list the maximum number of beds available. Generally speaking, the larger the party, the less the expense per person. Other details about the property and the conditions of renting are detailed in the promotional material.

You can find listings in guides from the British Tourist Authority and bookstores in the U.S. and Canada. The classified section of magazines such as *British Heritage* has ads for rentals. You can also find ads for self-catering accommodations in the Sunday editions of British newspapers. The *Sunday Times* and the *Observer* are available at newsstands in major American cities.

Other options include home exchanges; renting a *caravan* (trailer) in a *holiday park*; staying in a farmhouse; and a variety of specialty accommodations linked to a particular sporting or leisure activity such as skiing, fishing or *shooting* (hunting).

Your first resource for more information about these options is the British Tourist Authority.

Chapter Seventeen

FOOD AND TEA

"There are in England sixty different religious sects, but only one sauce."
Prince Francesco Caracciolo (1752-1799)

Britain is not considered by most Americans as their automatic choice for a gourmet vacation. However, it is no longer fair to say the fog in Britain is due to the over boiling of potatoes. British culinary standards, both in homes and restaurants, have increased dramatically over the past quarter century.

Britain's unfortunate reputation for bland, unadventurous cooking dates from the Industrial Revolution when a massive shift of population from rural areas to the burgeoning new cities and towns occurred. Until then, Britain was primarily agricultural. Fresh fruits, vegetables, meats, herbs and spices were always available from farms and local markets.

Two things changed. First, many abandoned farming and went to work in cities so there was less fresh food available and secondly, the cost of transporting fresh food raised the cost beyond the means of workers.

Of course, if they wanted, the wealthy had a

cuisine as sumptuous as anything offered in France.

Today, as visitors to Britain you will find as wide a variety of choices and quality as anywhere in the world. If you have an opportunity to sample domestic cooking, you will be pleasantly surprised. Influenced by membership in the European Community and the waves of immigration in the past thirty years, even the simplest cook dabbles with herbs and spices, garlic and olive oil. A glass of wine is ten times more likely to accompany a meal than it was in the 1960s.

A new generation of cooks is willing to experiment with strange new vegetables and exotic fruits. The older generation may have survived on boiled Brussels sprouts and baked apples but not any more.

Restaurants in Britain have imported some of the world's finest chefs. Even the notoriously bland motorway restaurants have improved.

More recent demographic and social changes have meant food shopping patterns have altered, too. For years, Britons relied on the little local food stores - grocers, bakers, butchers and greengrocers - for nearly all their food requirements. In some inner city communities, especially those with large ethnic populations, the local store may still be the place to shop. In other places, local indoor or outdoor markets provide fresh produce.

Supermarkets are the main source of provisions

for most people. During the 1980s and 1990s, many of these markets moved out of their High Street locations into out-of-town malls and shopping centres. They now offer an ever-increasing variety of items, including excellent prepackaged meals. Low inflation allows retailers to keep prices down.

Compared to people of the U.S. and Canada, the British are less apt to eat out except on special occasions such as birthdays and anniversaries. When you get your first check at a British restaurant, you'll see why.

Going out for breakfast is not as popular as it is in America. Britons generally enjoy breakfast at home so restaurants specializing in breakfasts are few and far between. That's a shame. Traditional English breakfast is a special treat.

Note: Before you reserve your hotel, ask if they serve a full English breakfast or if they have joined the growing army of establishments offering only "continental" breakfast.

Your full English breakfast will start with a bowl of cereal and a glass of fruit juice. The main course of bacon and/or sausage and eggs with mushrooms, fried tomatoes and fried bread will follow. (British bacon is usually much leaner than American bacon.)

Black pudding (blood pudding) may be offered.

Toast and marmalade or jam will follow. They may transport the toast to your table in a "toast rack." This means it will be cold when it arrives - normal in Britain.

Tea and coffee will be provided. You may have to ask for a refill - it doesn't happen automatically.

As an alternative to bacon and eggs, some restaurants offer kippers, lamb chops or even kidneys as your main course.

Continental breakfast usually consists of a roll and butter accompanied by butter or margarine and a beverage of your choice.

If you feel *peckish* (hungry) during the morning and feel desperate for a doughnut, off to the local bakers you must go. Once there, you will find an underwhelming choice of three varieties. Choose one with jam in the middle, one without jam in the middle or one with no middle at all.

Don't despair! You'll soon be tempted by the array of alternatives. Try a Chelsea bun or a slice of lard cake.

Sunday lunch is something special. Traditionally, it is the time when families and friends get together. The menu is most often a roasted meat. You may see lamb with mint sauce; pork with apple sauce; beef (sliced thin) with Yorkshire pudding; or poultry with stuffing. Crispy roast potatoes are staple fare. They are served with two other vegetables, baked or boiled. There is lots of gravy to smother the meat - and any other portion of the meal.

Many hotels and pubs run *carveries* if you don't have the opportunity to sample a traditional Sunday lunch with a British family. These consist of a roast buffet style with a variety of *starters* (first courses), a main course as described above and a choice of traditional *puddings* (dessert) such as apple pie. (You will be encouraged to drown your pie with hot custard sauce.) Carvery meals frequently give you exceptional value.

Most of the up-market restaurants ask for reservations in advance. If you go into a restaurant without a reservation, they will ask you to wait for a table - just like in America.

Once seated, you will be greeted by Doris, your friendly caring waitress. She will give you a menu and a wine list to peruse and ask if you want an *aperitif.* Doris will give you ample time to think about what you want to eat. When she returns to take your order, chances are she won't understand a word you say and you don't have a clue to what she is talking about. After some effort, you get your message across to each other. Depending on the attitudes of the waitress and you, this can be a fun experience or anger provoking.

Doris may be visibly irritated by your request for a jug of water but you won't be served water unless you ask for it.

The Brits have not yet been persuaded into the custom of serving a salad with a meal so if you want one, you must order it separately. Your salad will be served with your main course, not before it. The restaurant may have only one type of dressing, not the wide array you are used to at home.

After your first course arrives - it should take no longer than fifteen minutes - you'll find your conversation and your meal interrupted every ten minutes by the return of Doris (a recycled British Airways hostess). She will ask, "Is everything alright?"

Being a forthright American, you'll tell her your chicken is raw, the French fries are burnt to a cinder and your son intends to use the peas as ammunition for his peashooter.

Meanwhile, your British friends continue to eat without complaint. British people are as shy in restaurants as they are in shops and stores. Brits frequently *apologize* to the waiter for leaving some of the meal - as if he cares.

The British, like most Europeans, use knife and fork in conjunction. The fork is used to pin down the morsel while the knife is used to cut it up. Using your fork only is a dead giveaway that you are an American.

After the main course, an appealing (or appalling, depending on the restaurant) array of desserts will be brought to your table on a *trolley* (cart). Or, you might prefer to indulge in the civilized and venerable habit of following your meal with a slab of Stilton or other British cheese, crackers and a glass of fine port.

Tipping has long been a source of controversy in Britain. Many *bills* (checks) will include a service charge - usually 10%. Any tip above the service charge is entirely discretionary. Hotel and restaurant workers are notoriously low paid so if your waiter has been courteous, efficient and attentive, an additional tip is much appreciated.

England's roast beef with Yorkshire pudding and Scotland's *haggis* (a sheep's stomach bag stuffed with spiced liver, offal, oatmeal and onion) are about as close as you get to a national dish. Other meals popular with the Brits are steak and kidney pie; *bangers* (sausage) and *mash* (mashed potato); *bubble and squeak* (leftover potatoes and cabbage fried in a pan); *toad-in-the-hole* (sausages buried alive in soft batter).

Then there are *fish and chips* (french fries). The fish is usually cod or plaice (flatfish). After frying, the whole serving is doused with malt vinegar. It is served in a conically shaped paper container to carry out.

Potatoes are cooked and served in a multitude of different ways.

A cause of consternation to Americans is the

British fondness for Marmite - a thick brown yeast spread. It is smeared sparingly on bread or toast for a snack.

Since the influx of New Commonwealth and Caribbean immigrants in the 1950s and 1960s and Britain's membership in the European Community in 1970, the quantity and quality of Britain's ethnic food scene has rapidly expanded.

You will find Chinese and Indian restaurants in about every High Street - and even in country villages. The diversity of regional cooking within these countries is reflected in their menus. The tendency is to *Anglicize* the cuisine so you may find curries you expect to be spicy hot to be mild beyond recognition.

Look at the customers before you decide to eat. If you see Indians eating in an Indian restaurant, there is a good chance the food is delicious.

In fact, Indian food seems to be capturing the imagination of once conservative British palates. More than 2.5 million Indian meals are consumed in 8,000 Indian and Asian restaurants every week in what has been described as a "tidal wave of curry." Curry is now as British as tripe and onions. Heat-and-serve Indian meals are big business generating over £100 million in profits per annum.

French and Italian restaurants are popular. Italian dishes lend themselves to the *takeaway* (takeout) concept. Italian pizzeria and pasta joints now compete with MacDonald's and home-grown Wimpy for the fast food trade. The *doner kebab* is another popular takeaway food. Additional popular ethnic foods include Greek, Afro-Caribbean, Japanese and Thai.

Tea *" . . .everything stops for tea. "*

Ask the majority of Brits if they like Lapsang Souchong or Oolong and they will tell you, "I've never met them." Despite having stomachs coated with tannin, Brits are not the great experts on tea you may have assumed them to be. They'd much rather rely on familiar mass-produced "safe" blends than bother with all that foreign stuff. They most often buy Typhoo, Brooks Bond P.G. or a supermarket in-house brand.

Though they may not be tea gourmets, tea is an obsession with Brits. A pleasing *cuppa* tea anytime day or night is sure to make any Brit feel better.

Tea drinking in Britain became fashionable in the early 1700s. Tea houses, mainly for ladies appeared in London to rival the male dominated coffee houses of the period. Gradually, tea drinking gained the popularity it has today.

Any Briton will tell you it was the *cuppa*, not Winston Churchill, that got Britain through two world wars.

Why tea? Is there some secret ingredient? Is it

an excuse for British workers to stop work for a few minutes? Is it a reminder of the days of Empire, when Britain ruled the waves - and most of the world's tea plantations? The answer is probably a mixture of all three.

Tea is a national panacea for all ills, bringing a smile to the face of a burly bricklayer or a frail nonagenarian. Whether served in an elegant bone china cup or a cracked Charles and Di wedding souvenir mug, tea keeps Britain going - in every sense of the word.

The key to making an excellent cup of tea is an ancient ritual. Make sure the inside of the tea pot is tannin-stain free. Warm the pot by filling with hot water. When your tea water is boiling, empty the warming water from the pot. Add fresh tea leaves (one teaspoonful for each cup and one for the pot is the general rule). Pour in *boiling* water. Allow the tea to steep for five minutes. Brits cover the pot with a tea cosy to keep the beverage hot while it is steeping.

Britons claim the best invention ever is the electric kettle. In it, you can boil three pints of water in about four minutes.

You can divide Brits into two camps - those who add milk to their cups before the tea is poured (prelactarians) and those who add milk after the tea is poured (postlactarians). There are endless debates on the subject but what *is* certain is that milk is nearly always added to tea in Britain.

The average Briton consumes eleven cups a day and tea is drunk at all times of the day but tea-time comes around four in the afternoon. A pot - or more likely these days, a mug - may be accompanied by *biscuits* (cookies), crumpets or buttered toast and jam (or cheese, as my grandfather preferred).

High tea is more elaborate and usually involves a cooked meal.

Two British experiences to cherish - take afternoon tea in a country garden on a warm Summer's day. Relish the freshly made tea served with scones, jam and clotted cream. Take tea at one of the great hotels (London's *Brown's* or *Ritz* or Edinburgh's *Balmoral*). It's an experience you will never forget. You can choose from a remarkable variety of brews served with delicately cut finger sandwiches with cucumber, salmon, eggs or many other fillings. Don't miss this!

When you visit a British home, they will hand a cup of tea to you - almost before you have time to plonk yourself in a chair. You will be offered another - then another. Your host will say, "I think I can squeeze a tiny drop more out of the pot. Will you have some more?"

Coffee is popular in Britain, especially in the morning, but nothing can break the stranglehold of tea.

Chapter Eighteen

THE CULTURE

"There is something remarkable and peculiarly English about the passion for sitting on damp seats watching open-air drama."
Sheridan Morley, Critic

Artistic and cultural activity in Britain ranges from the highest professional standards to a variety of amateur efforts. London, the focus of cultural life, is one of the world's leading centers for drama, music, opera and dance.

Other towns and cities in Britain are cultural centers of significant achievement. Edinburgh is host to the world's largest cultural event, the Edinburgh International Festival. They hold it in August and the first part of September.

Glasgow is still reeling in delight from its coronation as Europe's 1990 Capital of Culture.

Manchester, Birmingham, Cardiff and a host of other cities offer artistic excellence.

Theatre

Americans and Canadians wax lyrical about the British theatre, even if the Brits themselves don't. The British have a quaint custom of undervaluing everything they do well. It extends to the theatre.

Britain has about three hundred theatres intended for professional use. About one hundred of those are in London.

London's theatre life is centered - but by no means confined - in the famous West End where the byword is choice. You can enjoy productions by the Royal Shakespeare Company at the Barbican Centre and the National Theatre Company at the South Bank Complex.

Revel in selections such as jolly musicals by Andrew Lloyd-Webber and Steven Sondheim; plays by British writers John Mortimer and Alan Ayckbourn; bawdy romps inspired by popular TV sitcoms; variety shows starring popular singers - they are all here.

If the West End is London's equivalent of Broadway, then the London fringe theatres are the equivalent of off-Broadway. Here, budding new bards get a chance to strut their stuff.

Such is the selection, it is important for you to pick carefully. I've known whole groups of Americans to come away from a play disappointed, baffled and bored. The accents and terminology are so integral to understanding the plot that the whole point of the play is lost to anyone but the Britons in the audience.

Theatre tickets are available at many agencies all over the city. (Don't pay over the top prices to ticket sharks.) At Leicester Square's ticket booth you can buy last-minute, same day tickets. You may have to *queue* (stand in line) for them.

Most of London's theatres are small - around 500 seats - and laid out in tiers with the stalls occupying the main floor and various circles above. *Playbills* (programs) are available before performances and during the *interval* (intermission). Many theatres have bars open before the performance begins. You can order your interval drinks in advance so you don't have to queue later.

London is home to two major opera houses, the Royal Opera House and the English National Opera.

The Sadler's Wells Royal Ballet is based in Birmingham. In Glasgow you'll find the Scottish Opera and the Welsh National Opera is based in Cardiff.

Once upon a time going to the theatre, a concert or an opera demanded some degree of formality. Dress codes still linger in places like Covent Garden. However, the invasion of London, Stratford and other major theatre centers by casually dressed tourists has led to an easing of codes. When you take into account that most British theatres are not air-conditioned this is not a bad thing. On a hot Summer day, a seat "in the gods" can be more like a seat in Hades when you are wearing a jacket and tie.

The Pantomime is a unique British theatre phenomenon. Pantomimes are costumed musical comedies with a great deal of slapstick. They usually star well-known TV personalities and are built around the theme of a child's story such as *Jack in the Beanstalk* or *Aladdin*. Pantomimes are primarily intended for children but seem just as popular with their parents. The pantomime season starts just before Christmas and extends into January - much as the season for the *Nutcracker* does in the U.S.

Films

Brits have been in love with films for a long time but gone are the days when going to the *pictures* (movies) was more popular here than anywhere else in the world. Cinema attendance reached its peak in 1946 with a total attendance of more than sixteen hundred million, then plummeted to a little over fifty million visits by 1985. In the mid-1990s the signs of recovery are unmistakable.

Downtown and suburban cinemas can be found in most British cities but the modern Brit is likely to visit an out-of-town shopping center for cinematic pleasure. Multi-screen movie houses mushroomed during the mall building blitz of the 80s and 90s.

Britain's hard-up film industry has seen better days but British films, actors, creative and technical services are acclaimed at international film festivals. The BBC or Channel 4 commission some of the best productions. Things are looking up.

Television and Radio

The BBC is one of the largest broadcasting companies in the world - almost certainly the largest government owned broadcasting company.

The BBC was founded in 1927. There are no commercials on BBC television or radio. *Every* television owner in Britain pays an annual license fee whether or not they watch TV. The government dispatches dozens of *detector vans.* They prowl the streets seeking out homes where people are watching television to check if their fee is paid.

The BBC is regarded as a public service. It is obligated to provide impartial news and current affairs coverage as well as sports and entertainment. For this reason, as well as Britain's greater dependence on the outside world, its coverage of international news is considerably more extensive than the American media's international coverage.

It is managed by a permanent staff, who are in turn overseen by a Board of Governors appointed by the government.

With some notable exceptions (such as the occasional rejection of interviews with members of terrorist organizations) the government keeps its distance.

With a strict ban on advertising, the BBC has been known to go ridiculously out of its way to avoid any semblance of commercial bias. On one popular child's show, brand names were covered by *plasters*

(Band-Aids) on items being used for handicrafts.

There are questions about whether the BBC's policy of producing quality programming not dictated by market requirements can survive in an era when global players like ABC/Disney or Time/Warner are increasingly calling the tunes. The question is; can the BBC survive as a public sector organization barred by regulation and its own culture from acting independently?

Long gone are the days when dear, old Auntie BBC dominated the airwaves. Since 1950 there has been ITV (Independent Television) exposing Britons to commercials for the first time. ITV is regarded as more down market than the BBC though one of its earlier successes, the soap opera *Coronation Street* is the most popular show on television today. It is watched by more than 17 million people.

ITV's staples include variety shows, game shows, quizzes, situation comedies, dramas, current affairs programs, children's programs and documentaries. ITV is capable of producing fine costume drama, too. American imports make up a substantial slice of ITV's programming.

The news wing of ITV is the respected ITN (International Television News). Their international news stories are shown on a number of public television stations in the U.S.

These two channels were joined by BBC2 in 1967 and Channel 4 in the 1980s. Both are governed by the same Independent Broadcasting Authority.

They are all beamed by a nationwide system of transmitters into aerials (antennas). You can see them on the skyline of every British city.

The government has been talking for years about inaugurating a new terrestrial channel to be called Channel 5. It finally appeared in 1997.

The biggest threat to the BBC and the other channels comes not from the prospect of additional terrestrial channels but from the popular explosion of satellite TV.

From the 1980s onward, huge, ugly satellite dishes began to sprout on homes all over the country. Pizza pan sized dishes are beginning to replace them.

Most recently, cable networks are being laid the length and breadth of the country. They are bringing a new dimension to broadcasting with new channels and other on-line services.

By the year 2000, seven million homes out of a possible fifteen hundred million are expected to be wired to a cable TV service.

It remains to be seen whether the BBC has the guts to keep up by joining the fray, going international or - dare I say - going commercial.

Newspapers

In the relatively small country of Britain, national newspapers rather than regional ones, dominate the scene. About a dozen national dailies with southern, northern and Scottish editions are produced in London, Manchester, Edinburgh and Glasgow. They offer a diversity of political opinion and quality that seems to appeal to the world's most newspaper-friendly nation.

On the high end of the market, Britain has produced some of the finest broadsheet newspapers in the world. The *Times of London* is probably the most famous. The *Telegraph* and *Guardian* have fine reputations despite being at opposite ends of the political spectrum, right and left respectively.

In the middle of the quality range, popular papers are the *Mail* and the *Express.* They are printed in tabloid form but are generally less controversial than their down market rivals.

Britain has long been the bastion of a free press. However, some mass circulation tabloids have come under growing criticism for pushing the limits of that freedom too far. There have been calls for some restriction.

Newspapers such as the *Star* and the *Sun* battle it out for numerical superiority. They seem to specialize in the latest whiff of scandal from the Palace or the sexual exploits of some famous star though they claim to be serious, national newspapers. The *Sun's* daily topless page 3 girl has become an institution and the butt (pardon the pun) of stand-up comedians.

Most of the national newspapers produce extra-thick Sunday versions, complete with pull-out magazines.

Local dailies are usually published Monday through Saturday in the larger towns and cities. They concentrate mainly on local and regional news and features with some of the latest national and international developments.

Many communities have weekly newspapers which specialize in local news and advertising.

Prominent American daily newspapers, such as *The New York Times* or the *Washington Post* may be available on the day they are published. Newsagents in central London and a few other large cities often have them. The *International Herald Tribune* is widely available.

Radio

Since the 1970s, British radio has burgeoned with specialist stations catering to a multitude of ethnic and religious tastes.

The BBC enjoyed a virtual monopoly of Britain's radio waves until the 1970s. It had four main radio stations; Radio 1, specializing in pop music; Radio 2, soft music; Radio 3, classical and Radio 4, news and current affairs. The famous BBC World Service broadcasts from Bush House in the Strand in about 40 languages to all over the world and to local radio stations in about 20 cities.

The IBA (Independent Broadcasting Authority

- governor of ITV) was given permission in the 1980s to broadcast commercial radio. Since then, the British radio scene has burgeoned with all kinds of new specialist stations catering to many of the country's ethnic and religious tastes. The national BBC radio channels continue to broadcast high quality programs.

Music

During your trip to Britain don't miss one of the greatest free treats. Attend a service of Choral Evensong at one of the great cathedrals. Times are usually posted outside or call the cathedral for information. You don't have to be an Episcopalian, or even a Christian, to attend. Most days of the week you'll be invited by an usher to sit in the choir stalls close to the singers. You will be transported to another world by the ethereal quality of the singing and the glorious surroundings of a medieval cathedral.

Cathedrals frequently offer recitals and concerts, also.

Britain's leading symphony orchestras include the London Philharmonic, the City of Birmingham Symphony, The Bournemouth Symphony, the Hallé (Manchester) and the Royal Scottish Orchestra.

There are also world-renowned chamber orchestras. An example is the Academy of St. Martins-in-the-Fields.

British classical music has its roots in the monastic institutions of the Middle Ages when plainsong dominated. As choral harmony developed, so did the use of instruments, including the organ.

Note: Take a look at the vast organs in the great cathedrals. Some of them are centuries old. Try to be there when one is being played or find out if there are recitals scheduled.

The use of musical instruments flourished in the middle ages. Royalty and other aristocrats employed musicians to play for them, both during banquets and in private audiences.

A most musical sovereign was that Merry Monarch, Henry VIII. When he was not chopping of the heads of his wives, he could be found busily composing sonnets and love songs for his ladies. He was proud of his voice and often sang his own compositions at the court. During the Tudor period folk music flourished and cathedral music reached its pinnacle. Composers Thomas Tallis and his pupil William Byrd were dominant.

Both the composition and the performance of music were frowned upon during the Puritan Commonwealth in the mid-seventeenth century. More than the monarchy was restored in 1660 when Charles II became king. Music was fashionable again. Court musician Henry Purcell's music has endured for three centuries (they celebrated his tercentenary in 1995). Handel, a German composer enamored of London, became one of the greatest composers Britain has ever nurtured.

The nineteenth was a century of great hymn-writers and Gilbert and Sullivan produced their works. Sullivan produced fine hymn music, also.

The twentieth century has been the most active yet. Elgar, Vaughan Williams, William Walton and Benjamin Britten have had a huge impact on world music.

Don't forget Britain's contribution to contemporary music and jazz. The "British Invasion" was led by the best known group, the Beatles. Their music swept North America in the 1960s and they are still popular today. Individual vocalists and instrumentalists such as, Elton John, Rod Stewart, Phil Collins, David Bowie and Eric Clapton and others, have had an immense impact on North America. Bands like The Rolling Stones, The Who and Pink Floyd continue to be revered.

The survivors from this list and American performers are often on tour in Britain. The megastars frequently appearing in Wembley Stadium and other major venues.

Literature

Britain's literary heritage revolves around William Shakespeare - the Bard. His birthplace in Stratford-on-Avon and the new Globe Theatre on London's South Bank are musts on the itinerary of millions of tourists every year.

Note: The new Globe Theatre opened in 1997. It is a replica of the original Globe Theatre that once stood nearby.

Even without Shakespeare, English literature is the richest in the world. The polyglot origins of the English language have produced the largest vocabulary of any world tongue. Thus, the language can produce more nuances of mood and meaning than any other can convey.

The Anglo-Saxon Chronicles were written in Old English during the time of Alfred the Great. The Middle English of Geoffrey Chaucer followed them. His *Canterbury Tales* have captured the imagination of every generation since the time they wrote them.

Development of the printing press and increased literacy helped popularize literature. Besides Shakespeare, Christopher Marlowe and Sir Thomas More characterized the Tudor era.

Ben Jonson's satirical comedies were written during the Jacobean period. A group of metaphysical poets, led by John Donne, Dean of St. Paul's Cathedral, published their work. The King James, or authorized version of the Bible was first published.

During the Commonwealth, serious authors John Milton and John Bunyan dominated the literary scene. After the restoration, a more relaxed atmosphere was receptive to the writings of Sheridan and Samuel Pepys.

The next century is dominated by Dr. Samuel Johnson. He is famous for his *Dictionary of the English Language* and a host of letters and essays. Other great writers of the century include Daniel Defoe, Henry Fielding and Oliver Goldsmith.

The early 19th century glittered with a stellar array of outstanding writers - Blake, Shelley, Wordsworth, Coleridge, Byron, Keats and Austin. Scotland produced the work of Robert Burns and Sir Walter Scott.

The mid to late 1900s saw even more giants - Dickens, Tennyson, the Brontes, Lewis Carroll, Thomas Hardy, Mathew Arnold and, going into the twentieth century - Kipling, H.G. Wells, Somerset Maugham and Dylan Thomas.

Note: Many travel companies feature tours of the birthplaces or homes of famous literary figures. You can visit Dylan Thomas' study in Laugharne, Wales, Thomas Hardy's cottage in Higher Bockhampton, Dorset and the home of Sir Walter Scott near Edinburgh in Scotland.

The British Library (a new national library) is soon to be completed in London. It will be one of the world's three largest. Scotland's National Library is in Edinburgh and the Welsh National Library is located in Cardiff.

Museums

Britain has 2,500 museums and art galleries. Some of them are among the world's finest - not surprising in a country that ruled a world wide empire.

London is the hub of museum and art gallery activity. World class institutions such as the British Museum, the National Gallery, the Victoria and Albert Museum and the Tate Gallery are legendary for the quality and quantity of the material they possess. Despite their vastness, what is on show is only the tip of the iceberg. The majority of items are hidden from public view.

Many larger cities have important museums and art collections. Birmingham's Art Gallery specializes in the work of the pre-Raphaelites. Oxford's Ashmolean Museum is of the standard you would expect in one of the world's most prestigious centers of learning. In addition, the National Gallery of Scotland in Edinburgh, the Burrell Collection in Glasgow and the Fitzwilliam in Cambridge merit your attention.

Private collections of literature and art are often on display in sumptuous surroundings. For example, see some of the Queen's art collection in the Queen's Gallery.

Don't miss visiting stately homes. They are treasure troves, not only of paintings, but of furniture, architecture and often, landscaping.

Chapter Nineteen

PUBS

"Come, come and have a drink with me/ Down at the old Bull and Bush."
Song by Harry Tilzer

After the Royal family, perhaps the best known British institution is the pub - short for public house. Imitations may have appeared all over the world, including North America, but nowhere do they quite capture the unique atmosphere of their British forebears.

Pubs can be found everywhere - remote villages, heavily populated industrial suburbs and busy downtown commercial areas. Even tiny villages may have several.

There is a pub for just about every mood and occasion. There are pre-theatre pubs, gay pubs, geriatric pubs, gay geriatric pubs, pre-bingo pubs, post-bingo pubs, pubs for journalists, shoppers - you name it.

Pubs may be noisy, rowdy and energetic or so peaceful you can hear a pin drop. Pubs are *the* place to see the British at play, to people watch and to make friends. You may be surprised at how easy it is to make acquaintances among the normally reserved Brits over a warm pint of beer at the "local." If you

215

happen into a pub not your style, just drink up and move onto the next one. It won't be far away.

Historically, pubs have their roots in the ancient hostelries or taverns used by pilgrims and other travelers. With travel slow and hard, people often stayed a night or two while enroute to medieval shrines or visits to other parts of the country. Commercial travelers plying their wares along the cross-county highways such as the Great West or Great North Roads stayed at the inns or taverns regularly. Generally, pubs are no longer hostelries.

The intriguing names given to pubs usually give a hint of their historical roots. The name may commemorate a legendary event or be the result of a distortion of the original name.

For example, in Trollope's book, *Framley Parsonage*, the title of chapter 32 is the name of a pub, *The Goat and Compasses*. He writes, ". . .a few hundred yards down a cross-street he came to a public-house. It was called the *Goat and Compasses* - a very meaningless name, one would say; but the house boasted of being a place of public entertainment very long established on that site, having been a tavern out in the country in the time of Cromwell. At that time, the pious landlord, putting up a pious sign for the benefit of his pious customers, had declared that "God Encompasseth Us." The Goat and Compasses in these days does quite as well; and, considering the present character of the house, was perhaps less unsuitable than the old legend."

The King and Tinker pub in Enfield, north London was already in existence under another name in the early 1600s. King James I is said to have stopped for a pint during a hunting expedition. He chatted with a local tinker while drinking. Such a "prince and pauper" tale caught the imagination of the local folk so they renamed the pub to commemorate the event.

In the Middle Ages, large cities such as London, Norwich and Bristol attracted many people from outlying districts to the regular market days. Pubs became a focus of city and town life. They occasionally offered accommodations.

With the huge increase in the British population following the Industrial Revolution, pubs began to appear in the new suburbs and the "local" was born.

Pubs had become such an essential part of the British social fabric that, during World War II when road signs were removed, people would give directions to non-German strangers in terms of the local pubs.

During the 1960s and 70s large brewery conglomerates took over more and more of the local establishments. As a result, much "streamlining" took place. Long, oak mirrored bars and original brass fittings were replaced by wood veneer, Formica and other tacky materials. This provoked a movement to preserve the more historic pubs. It has had some success.

Whatever the furnishings are like, the most important facet of the pub is the *people* who frequent it. In Britain, a pub is a center of community social life. It is unlike virtually every other institution in that it seems like an extension of your living room.

Neighborhood locals generally mirror the people who live in the immediate vicinity. The atmosphere in a middle-class suburban pub is likely to be quite different from that of a pub in an industrial suburb of Coventry, for example.

A downtown pub at lunchtime will reflect the people who work or shop in the surrounding district. At night, when the nearby shops and businesses are closed, the same pub may attract a completely different crowd.

Americans unfamiliar with pubs may be amazed at the variety of customers. Singles, *doubles* (couples), whole soccer teams and elderly women exchanging gossip over a Marks and Spencer carrier bag can all be found in a pub.

Most pubs possess their share of characters. Its no coincidence that Britain's two most popular soap operas, regularly watched by almost a quarter of the total population, revolve around life in their neighborhood pubs. Watch *Coronation Street* with its pub *Rover's Return* and *East Enders* with the *Queen Vic*.

Pubs are usually divided into two or three bars.

Generally speaking, the public bar is the place to enjoy a spot of snooker or darts in a noisy, smoky environment. It will have basic furnishings, "spit and sawdust" style.

The lounge bar will be a little more luxurious and a good deal quieter, though you still may be able to cut the thick smoke in the air with a pair of scissors.

There has been a recent growth in the "pub grub" industry. More and more pubs serve lunch and even evening meals, all at much lower cost than most restaurants - filling a vacuum in the British market - and stomach.

Traditional pub fare such as Plowman's Lunch (a chunk of cheese, usually Cheddar; a crusty roll with butter and a pickled onion or two) or dainty, British style sandwiches sprinkled with mustard and cress retain their popularity. A growing number of pubs offer hot meals, snugly served in a basket.

Many pubs also claim to offer tea, coffee and other hot drinks. During busy periods the bartender is likely to strongly hint he is not at all happy about having to make you a perfectly-brewed, piping hot cup of Earl Grey while people on the other end of the bar are waiting for their pint of warm, frothy bitter.

One of the most confusing aspects of the British pub scene for North American visitors is the opening hours. This has long been a topic of debate among the British themselves. Pub opening times were trimmed back during the First World War because of concerns about night lighting during the blackout and military personnel getting "sloshed."

Pubs were also closed afternoons. Sunday opening hours were restricted, largely due to the powerful influence of the established church. It deemed drinking alcohol on Sundays to be particularly sinful.

Until recently, despite fifty years of relative peace, little had been done to revise the law. A change in the law in 1988 allowed pubs to remain open during the afternoon. No attempt was made to extend the closing time beyond the conservative 11:00 P.M. At that time, the landlord rings a loud, clanging bell and screams, "Time, gentlemen, please." After the bell is rung, you cannot order more drinks but there is an additional ten minutes drinking up time before you are asked, gently at first - then more aggressively - to leave.

Sometimes, on special occasions, pubs apply to local magistrates for an extension allowing them to stay open until midnight or even later. Extensions are granted for special occasions such as the Queen's silver jubilee celebration or the D Day 50th Anniversary celebrations.

A liberalization of the Sunday trading laws occurred in the mid-1990s and pubs are now allowed to stay open all day Sundays. This brought Britain in line with the rest of Europe. Nevertheless, most pubs still close at 11 P.M.

Those wishing to continue drinking after eleven must wend their way to one of the "drinking clubs," discos, nightclubs or wine bars. Some of these, depending on the local magistrates, stay open until 1:00 A.M., 2:00 A.M. or even later. A cover charge may be required. In the case of a member's club, you may be asked to pay a membership fee and, sometimes, furnish identification.

Another matter of consternation for the North American visitor will be the public drinking habits of the British. Upon arrival in a pub, the first hurdle is to find a place to sit or stand. Standing for several hours is considered quite acceptable.

Pubs virtually never have waiter/waitress service. Don't make the mistake of sitting at your table waiting for that pleasant young person to come over and attend to you. If the pub is busy, you may have to fight your way to the bar, attract the barman or barmaid's attention. Surprisingly, a five-pound note is more likely to get attention than a fifty-pound note.

While you are waiting, decide what you want. The sheer variety of types of alcoholic beverages is enough to confuse even an expert.

If you are with British people in a pub, buying a round of drinks for everyone in the group is customary. If, by chance, you are with the entire chorus of "Sunset Boulevard," people will likely club together to buy a round - unless Andrew Lloyd

Webber is paying.

Asking for a "beer" in Britain is a bit like asking for a "drink." Beer is a very broad term. You need to be specific about what type of beer you want. The yellow beer seen most frequently in the U.S. is known as lager in Britain. As in the U.S., they serve it cooled and it is available on draft, bottled or canned. If you feel really homesick, American and Canadian brews - Budweiser, Coors and Labatt's - are widely available.

In a country considerably less smitten with choice, you may be surprised to find yourself being asked what kind of glass you'd like to drink from - with or without a handle. Some say the shape of the glass can actually affect the taste of the beer.

Darker beers are often known as ales, but even this is a general term. Bitter, usually served on draft, refers to a darkish brown froth-crowned liquid. It has a strong, sharp taste. When applied to bitter, the terms "special" and "best" refer to strength, not quality. Pale and light ales are the bottled versions of bitter.

Mild, another brew, contains more sugar and is sweeter than pale or light. Stouts brews are made from well-roasted, unmalted barley. They are all very dark and sometimes sweet. Guiness, Ireland's most famous concoction, is thick and rich like all stout, but not sweet.

Many North Americans are horrified to discover that darker beers are served warm. "Warm" really means room temperature. Like a good red wine, keeping the beer at room temperature means they satisfy your taste buds to the maximum.

The British pub industry won an important concession in 1995. While all other liquid measurements (gas, milk, etc.) must by European Community law be measured in litres, beers, lagers and other ciders may still be sold in pints. Be specific when you order. Say, "A pint o' bitter, please." Or, "Half o' lager, please." Bottled beers usually come by the half-pint. Just ask for, "a bottle o' (brand name)." Increasingly, non-alcoholic beers and lagers are found in pubs.

Another popular drink in Britain is cider. It is served by the pint or half when on draft and also in bottles and cans. Unlike its harmless American counterpart, a mainstay at children's parties, most English cider contains alcohol in both its sweet and dry forms. The more murky the cider is, the stronger it is. In the West Country, Herefordshire and Gloucestershire where cider is made, some local producers manufacture "scrumpy" - a rough, murky, *powerful* cider. Be warned!

The British rarely talk of "cocktails" unless they are referring to a pre-dinner drinks party - or unless they have spent time in America. Even then, the invitation, "Do come round for cocktails." means gin and tonic, scotch and dry or a remarkably crude Bloody Mary. You won't find the unpronounceable cocktails invented in the U.S.

If you *are* desperate for a Harvey Wallbanger, probably you can get one in the bar at your hotel. Don't be surprised if it tastes quite different from what you are accustomed to back home. They may attribute the discrepancies to the different system of liquid measurements or, sometimes, the incompetence/inexperience of the bar staff.

Popular pub "shorts" include gin (produced mainly in England) and usually served with tonic water or whisky (*uisige beathe* in Gaelic literally meaning, "the water of life.") Whisky has been produced in Scotland for centuries. It is one of the nation's top exports, worth well more than $3 billion a year.

There are two main types: malt whisky, which uses only malted barleys and grain whisky, made with other cereals. A single malt is the product of a single distillery. Blended whisky, as its name infers, is a blend of malt and grain whiskies.

The standard measure in pubs is a measly one sixth of a gill. Given this meagre measure, it's not surprising many choose to add water, ginger ale, orange or some other concoction to their tipple. You'll be mocked and ridiculed if you add anything but Highland water to your malt, especially north of the border - it's unthinkable!

As your barman pushes your glass up to the inverted bottle on the wall and places it down on the counter, you may be forgiven for believing it is empty. Look again. The drink is there - somewhere. If you ask for ice, remember "scotch on the rock" is a more accurate description of what you are likely to be given when you order "scotch on the rocks."

In Scotland, don't ask for scotch at all - ask for whisky. Most pubs on both sides of the border provide ice buckets at the bar. Don't hesitate to help yourself - if the ice hasn't melted, that is.

The rule for tipping is *don't*. Tipping the bar staff in a British pub is unheard of. If you are so moved, you might offer him/her a drink, however. This is a common practice, especially after a few rounds have been downed. Any episode of *Coronation Street* will show you that.

In many of the larger pubs with several rooms, whole areas are often set aside for indoor sports, especially darts, possibly *skittles* (a rustic form of ten-pin bowling), snooker (the transatlantic granddaddy of pool), dominoes, tiddlywinks and, more often than not, a juke box.

Live music by local jazz or rock bands is an evening feature of many pubs. Pubs virtually never require an entrance fee, even when live entertainment is provided. In the unlikely event you come across a pub holding a strip show, you might be asked for a cover charge. What they'll cover is anybody's guess. Friday and Saturday are generally the busiest nights in a pub. Friday is traditionally payday.

Note: Do not expect to engage in the art of conversation if a band is playing in a pub.

Many hostelries, both in city and country, possess beer gardens. They can provide a pleasant location on a sunny Summer afternoon or on the three nights of the British summer when it is warm enough to sit *al fresco*. Even then you might find yourself fighting off the gnats or midges who want to enjoy the fine weather with you.

Beer gardens frequently have children's amusements, such as swings and slides. Sometimes they have other attractive features like live goats, pigs or other farmyard animals.

Unless there is a special outside bar, drinks are normally purchased inside. This can be hazardous, particularly if you are carrying out a large round. Bar meals can usually be brought outside.

If, despite all this talk about pubs, you still prefer to drink in the relative safety and privacy of your own room, alcohol can be purchased in many hotels but expect to pay an exorbitant price for this luxury. You may want to buy a bottle or two from a supermarket or the British equivalent of the liquor store. Called an *off-license* or *offie* they were as much the victim of archaic opening hours as the pub until recently.

Another intriguing British custom is the pub crawl - an evening spent with friends (or enemies) travelling from one pub to another, then moving on the another and then another.

This custom is particularly popular on pre-wedding stag and hen nights. The despicable intention is to get the prospective groom or bride as drunk as possible. Since pubs are often within walking distance of one another and public transportation is generally good, the combination of drinking and driving is easily avoided.

A comparatively recent arrival on the British drinking scene is the wine bar. Although wine has been produced in Britain since Roman times, drinking it was another matter altogether. The British figured, albeit reluctantly, this was something the French did better. Consequently, most wine available in Britain is produced in mainland Europe but American and Australian wines are increasing in popularity by the minute.

Drinking wine was regarded as the prerogative of the aristocracy and upper middle classes for a long time. One of the benefits of Britain's membership in the European community is that wine is much cheaper than before, so drinking it has become more widespread. Though not as widely consumed *en famille* as in countries such as France and Italy, wine will often accompany a meal in a restaurant or at Sunday lunch - certainly on special occasions.

The wine bar is a product of this new age, owing more to European style bar than to the traditional pub. Wine bars tend to be frequented by young professionals and often suffer from an identity crisis. "Am I a bar or a restaurant?" they say. Nearly all wine bars serve meals. They tend to be more up-market than the meals served in pubs. Music and dancing may be a feature. Because wine bars have a greater emphasis on food than pubs, some of them have had greater success in being allowed to stay open until the wee hours.

British law states you may not purchase alcohol if you are under eighteen but U.S and Canadian visitors will be shocked to see young polka-dot faced people of tender age knocking back pint after pint with friends. The law also says you must not enter a pub if you are under the age of fourteen unless accompanied by an adult.

When a Brit is living in America, the feature of British life missed the most (apart from the BBC) is the pub. If you are nervous about entering one, do not fear! The combination of alcoholic beverage linked with the friendly atmosphere means that the average pub is a place where the British defrost as quickly as a packet of peas in a microwave.

A pub is a wonderful place for meeting or making friends. If you wish, you can be sociable or if you prefer to hide in a corner, no one will mind. Most importantly, no other place gives you a better glimpse into the everyday lives of the British. No other place is more likely to result in the making of friendships.

Since before the days of Chaucer, the pub has been a focal point - nay, *the* focal point of British community life and action. Like that other venerable British institution, "Long may she reign."

Note: The combination of drinking and driving, as in the U.S. and Canada, is frowned on in the U.K. Stiff penalties, sometimes including a night in a police cell, are frequently meted out to offenders who are "over the limit" when breathalized or otherwise examined. A sheepish look, an American accent along with the touristic claim, "I'm from Providence and I didn't know." is unlikely to evoke even the slightest sympathy.

P.S. *Never* talk religion or politics in a pub!

Cheers!

Chapter 20

SHOPPING

"England is a nation of shopkeepers."
Napoleon Bonaparte (quoting Adam Smith)

Britain is famous for its shopping, and rightly so. Most visitors to Britain are sooner or later enticed by the sheer variety and quality of merchandise available - even those who claim to detest shopping. They end up having to sit on their suitcase at the end of their trip to get it closed for the homebound journey.

Tacky souvenir shops selling the latest in Union Jack underwear and souvenir mugs abound in all the main tourist centers. Ignore them. The best items to take home are the classic quality items for which Britain is renowned - china and porcelain, crystal and glass, designer fashions, handicrafts, hats, rainwear, woolens, shoes and bagpipes.

The most noticeable difference between shopping at home and shopping in Britain is that much of the retailing (except for foods) still takes place downtown. The stores stir up nostalgic memories of Main Street USA before the automobile was elevated to the status of God.

Despite the best efforts of a string of

231

Conservative administrations to shift the focus of national transportation policy toward the private car, many Brits, sick and tired of cholesterolic traffic jams clogging their main arteries, still prefer to walk, take the bus or train into town. This is in spite of the mushrooming of large out-of-town shopping malls.

Another contributory factor in the survival of downtown shopping in Britain is the staggering (to Americans) fact that a large proportion of the population does not drive. Up and down the country, town and city authorities spend millions "pedestrianizing" downtown shopping areas. They divert cars, vans and trucks and enhance the streetscape with anaemic palm trees and hanging baskets of geraniums.

Ironically, in many cases the same authority is likely to be encouraging the construction of vast shopping complexes to be built on the urban fringes. More progressive councils have supported the building of malls in their downtown areas, complementing the existing mixture of national chain stores and smaller local outfits.

London's shops and stores are the envy of the world. The main shopping drag, Oxford Street, runs almost two miles east to west, from Tottenham Court Road to Marble Arch. It contains branches (sometimes several) of all Britain's chain stores. You'll find huge department stores like John Lewis, Selfridge's and Debenham's, as well as several indoor malls. Regent Street dissects Oxford Street at Oxford Circus. It is home to Liberty's department store and Hamley's toy emporium, always choc-a-bloc in the run up to Christmas.

Knightsbridge, barely a catapult fling from the western end of Oxford Street, is where you'll find Harrod's, the world's most famous department store and possibly its largest. They boast of being willing (and able) to sell you anything from a pair of hippos to a pin (who'd want to buy a pin?). The Harrod's food hall is one of the wonders of London.

Central London also boasts several specialty shopping areas. They range from the antique and fine arts stores around New Bond Street to Tottenham Court Road, the hi-fi enthusiast's heaven. Go to Savile Row for that perfect made-to-measure suit.

For a "nation of shopkeepers," British people are surprisingly docile when it comes to actually *doing* the shopping. In contrast to their more direct and aggressive American counterparts, most Brits *hate* to be approached by a sales assistant as soon as they enter a store. They are more content wasting hours looking for the object of their desire before "bothering" a member of staff with ridiculous questions about where they might find it. When they do ask, it's often done with an apologetic, "I'm so sorry to bother you, but..." When the sales assistant admits they do have the required item in stock, the prospective purchaser is completely aghast.

For most of the world, the act of queuing is almost as ludicrous as the spelling of the word. You'll find queuing is as much part of the British culture as fish and chips or afternoon tea. With its roots in the British obsession with fair play. It predates the First and Second World Wars by centuries. However, during the wars and postwar eras the formation of orderly lines for the limited rations available was an essential part of everyday life. "First come, first served" is as popular a principle in today's Britain as it ever was. Brits will form queues automatically - sometimes when they don't need to. Even thugs attending soccer games can be seen forming orderly queues in order to get into the stadium.

In the shops and stores queues are best observed. During the big January and summer sales, the practice is taken to extraordinary lengths. Sale items are usually advertized in the local paper in advance, often at a small percentage of the recommended retail price. Prospective purchasers will line up long before the sale is due to begin to be sure to get "their" purchase. Some have been known to camp out for days, relying on family and friends to bring them sustenance. It's pretty good P.R. for the store, too.

Note: If there is anything the British absolutely loathe, it's queue-jumping. Even when it's done by foreigners who don't know any better.

Food Shopping

Half a dozen major supermarket chains predominate in Britain of which the largest are Sainsbury's and Tesco. In most medium-sized towns, as well as the larger cities, you'll find at least one of them.

Newer, out-of-town stores usually have their own large *en suite* parking lots and public transport connections to other parts of town. At first sight, there's little difference between them and their North American cousins. They're clean (they have to be), they retail a vast range of goods and you'll feel at home with the layout.

As is often found, it's the little things that catch you out. When you enter the stores, you'll need to pick up a shopping basket (usually wire, not plastic), or a *trolley* (cart). As you peruse the shelves, you'll be impressed by the choice of merchandise, but not by the absence of many of your favorites from back home. Ranch dressing means no more to Brits than HP sauce does to you.

There's a staggering array of fresh produce, meat, fish and vegetables, including some unusual sights like *chidlings*, *winkles* (periwinkles) and tripe. Other familiar-looking items are labeled with different names, especially vegetables like *courgettes* (zucchini,) *Mange-tout* (snow peas) and *swede* (rutabaga). There's even a different vocabulary to describe the way the meat is cut.

With all perishable goods, check the expiration date, which by law must appear on the label. When purchasing pre-weighed goods, note the weight is now given only in kilos, so it pays to have a calculator handy. Most Brits are only just beginning to become familiar with the metric system.

Brits are no less health-conscious than Americans. You'll find a wealth of low-calorie, low-fat and low-cholesterol items to keep you happy. Vegetarians are also well cared for. Delicatessens feature in many of the larger supermarkets. Frequently, bread is baked on the premises, providing an enticing aroma.

One major difference in British supermarkets is the availability of high-quality, heat-and-serve meals (although they can be expensive). They cover the spectrum of gastronomic tastes - from shepherd's pie to chicken *tikka masala*. If you're ever near a Mark's and Spencer's food hall, you'll see what I mean.

British checkouts are lined with the same kind of titillating trash as most American and Canadian supermarkets, including "My Wife is an Alien" type tabloids and mouth-watering selections of *sweets* (candies). Empty the contents of your basket-trolley on to the conveyor, and the cashier will register them (in exactly the same way as at home).

Next comes the confusing part. Unlike American checkouts, once you've emptied the contents of your trolley on to the conveyor, you'll need to be ready *immediately* to put your purchases in the bag yourself - there's no one to pack the items for you. A carrier bag will be waved in your face by the cashier. Join the myriad of Brits who take their own beloved shopping bags - like appendages - along with them.

Payment is best made in cash, credit card, or a debit card embossed with one of the major credit card symbols.

Local Shops and Markets

Shopping in local stores can be a pleasure. In most small towns and villages in Britain you'll find at least a butcher, a baker, a fruiterer, a grocer, a fishmonger and an *ironmonger* (hardware store). You may pay more than you would at a supermarket, but you'll have the experience of dealing with a friendly, helpful staff and a chance to meet some of the locals. Plus, an opportunity to hear some of the local gossip!

An increasing number of small neighborhood stores are owned and run by members of various ethnic communities In many of Britain's inner-city areas, in addition to the regular stock, you'll discover an exotic array of provisions. Many of these stores offer the added bonus of staying open until late at night.

Bustling, colorful, noisy and great fun, markets can be found in just about every city and country town. They may be indoors, in purpose-built halls (especially in the north and midlands) or outside. Sometimes they are held in a market square used for the purpose for centuries. All manner of goods are sold, from fresh fish to frilly underwear, toys to toilet supplies. Raucous stall holders ply their wares in a cacophony of sights, sounds and smells.

London and some of the larger cities provide specialist markets dealing with specific types of goods. For example, Portobello Road and Camden Lock with their antiques and second-hand goods.

Yard sales as such do not exist in Britain. To start with, nobody owns a yard big enough to hold one, and, in any case, nobody would ever dream of keeping the proceeds for themselves.

Selling unwanted household items and clothes is the prerogative of churches and charitable institutions. Elderly ladies, who may otherwise display no religious inclination or affiliation, will save dozens of useless items. Then they send them to the local church for its *Jumble Sale*. Thus, they simultaneously ease their social conscience and provide sufficient credentials for membership in their local church.

Jumble sales normally take place on Saturday afternoons (or occasionally Friday evenings), most often in church halls. To find out which sales are operating any given Saturday, check the Friday night edition of the local paper. There will likely be a whole page of jumble sale advertisements. When the time comes for the sale, an orderly queue forms outside, but once the doors are opened, all hell lets loose!

From an American standpoint, it's fascinating enough just to wander round and see the trash that has been cluttering up local homes for years, not to mention the demonic behavior of normally very well-behaved, genteel pensioners. As an added incentive, you might stumble across an original Rembrandt or some other masterpiece of art that's been locked up in someone's attic for ages. Priceless antique treasures are frequently "discovered" at jumble sales!

Car Boot Sales have become popular over the past quarter-century. Vendors pay a fee to the organizer (which need not be a charitable institution), and then proceed to market the contents of their car's *boot* (trunk) - specially crammed for the occasion.

Charity shops operate on the same principle as jumble sales. Many people, especially young professionals, purchase their clothes second hand and ease their social conscience at the same time. They know the proceeds are being donated to organizations like Oxfam, Christian Aid or Help the Aged.

Apart from the traditional sales times, the most frenetic spell for shoppers is the six weeks or so leading up to Christmas. Up and down the country, brightly-colored illuminations adorn the streets, Christmas trees stand sentinel above virtually every shopfront. A thousand Father Christmases promise a million toys to wide-eyed boys and girls, accompanied by the mellifluous tones of Bing Crosby's *I'm Dreaming of a White Christmas.*

Shopping will never be a problem for you in the land where "lay away" means absolutely nothing. Just don't forget to queue!

Chapter Twenty-One

SPORTS

"Serious sport has nothing to do with fair play. It is bound up with hatred, jealousy, boastfulness, disregard of all rules and sadistic pleasure in witnessing violence. In other words, it is war minus the shooting."

Joe Orton: *The Sporting Spirit*

The Brits are proud of their sporting heritage-perfectly understandable for a nation that gave birth to soccer, golf, rugby, possibly tennis and, most proudly, cricket. Sporting heroes become national celebrities, but with a big price to pay. Their lives are inevitably put under a microscope by the tabloid press responding to an insatiable public thirst for "dirt."

Soccer

Americans will have to get used to Brits referring to the nation's most popular sport, soccer, as football. Despite several setbacks in recent years, it's still the game you'll see being played in every park and open space. Kids can be seen kicking the inflated pig's bladder (or a plastic substitute) around even in the concrete jungles of the inner cities.

Reverence for the game reached fever-pitch in 1966 when the English national team won the World

Cup (the most popular sporting event in the world) , at London's Wembley Stadium.

In 1990, England progressed to the semi-finals of the World Cup against Italy. Such was public interest in the game that during the half-time period the National Electricity Grid was barely able to keep up with the surge of power created by the switching on of millions of electric kettles at the same time. Simultaneously, the Water Authorities were deluged with the sudden demand for enough water to flush 25 million loos.

The name "soccer" derives from the Football Association, its governing body. It oversees the game in England and Wales. (Scottish football has a separate organization to manage its affairs.)

English and Welsh teams participate in a national league. The larger clubs slog it out in a forty-game championship division known as the Premiership. Smaller clubs battle it out in three lower divisions.

Scotland has its own competition, the Scottish League, dominated in its Premier division by old rivals, Catholic Celtic, and Protestant Rangers.

Players in the most popular teams both sides of the border, especially the more photogenic ones, earn huge salaries. Massive transfer fees are paid when a famous player moves from one club to another.

Note: The British, when referring to team membership, talk of being "in" not "on" a team.

All English and Welsh league clubs (and a number of non-league clubs who've made it through the qualifying rounds) contend for the annual Football Association Cup, commonly known as the F.A. Cup.

Traditionally held on the second Saturday in May, the final has roughly the same status and attracts the same amount of hype as the Superbowl. A separate Scottish Cup is held north of the border.

England, Scotland and Wales all have their own national teams. This means, in theory at least, Britain has at least three times as much chance of getting a team through to a European Championship or World Cup Final as any other nation.

English soccer's reputation has been marred in recent years by the appalling behaviour of some of its so-called "supporters." The behaviour reached its frenzied peak at the Heysel Stadium in Belgium, when Liverpool fans attacked rival supporters of the Italian club Juventus. Scores died in the tragedy. English clubs were thereby banned from European competitions for several years. Evidence linked much of the violence among the British soccer supporters to extreme right-wing political groups.

Another soccer tragedy took place in Sheffield, June 1, 1997. Dozens of supporters were crushed to death when the crowd surged forward during a game against Liverpool.

Attempts to restore soccer's tarnished

reputation have resulted in improvements in security and the upgrading of many of the country's stadiums - including the segregation of rival fans. League soccer is slowly but surely becoming a family game once again.

Even if you haven't a clue about what's going on, drop in on a match between two Premiership or Scottish Premier League clubs. It can be a thrilling experience, especially when it is a local derby (pronounced "darby") involving two clubs from the same city. You'll discover a vocabulary you never knew existed and see the British at their most passionate.

Cricket

Cricket is England's summer game (it never seems to have caught on in Scotland or Wales).

For many Americans, it is the most quintessentially English of sports. Slow, (international matches can last for up to five days), incredibly complicated (just take a look at the scoreboard) and very, very polite.

There is something oh, so English about seeing two teams of white-flanneled players contrasted against the lush hue of an idyllic village green, overlooked by an ancient parish church and majestic oak trees. The observers wait for the *whack* of the hard leather-coated ball against the willow of a cricket bat. Then, polite applause greets the scoring of a *run* or the fall of a *wicket*. Though not everyone's cup of tea, cricket is such an integral part of the English culture that it has produced everyday commonplace expressions like *a sticky wicket* and *knock for six.*

The modern game is said to date from the formation of the Hambledon Cricket Club in Hampshire. Its official rules were established in 1750, though its roots go back many centuries before (It took all that time to write the rules.)

It became a national game only after the foundation of the Lords' Cricket Ground in St. John's Wood, London (1814) and the subsequent formation of the Marylebone Cricket Club (the MCC), now the world governing body of cricket.

With the growth of Empire, cricket was exported all round the world. It is now a popular game in Australia, Pakistan, India, the West Indies, South Africa and New Zealand.

Today, cricket is played in schools and universities, in local parks, on sunny summer picnics and in local leagues comprising teams from pubs, factories and even clergy.

England's main cricket competition is the County Championship, dating from 1850. The cricket season starts in April and ends in September, overlapping for a few weeks with soccer. County matches are slated to last three days, unless rain stops play or a side is bowled out.

A separate Sunday league, much lambasted by the game's purists, involves much shorter games. These games have a much faster pace and higher scores. "It just isn't cricket!" the purists complain.

International games are held throughout the year and are usually called Test Matches. England's greatest cricket rival is Australia. (Scotland has never, wisely, taken to cricket) In 1878, the first Australian team to visit England beat the M.C.C. decisively, creating an intense rivalry and producing a unique phenomenon - a phantom trophy.

For most Americans, the *ashes* are cremated human remains or the family down the street. For most English and Australians, the *Ashes* is the title of the non-existent prize awarded to the winner of the best of five, five-day games between the two countries. The fact that Australia always seems to win prompted a famous British astronomer, Fred Hoyle, to comment that he could not look up into our galaxy without feeling that somewhere out there, *must* be a team that could beat the Australians!

Take time to study a game. (If you go to a game you will definitely have time to study it.) Preferably go with someone who can explain the rules to you. You'll notice cricket has a number of parallels with its young upstart nephew, baseball.

Rugby

Rugby is a winter game originating in 1823 in the famous public school at Rugby, Warwickshire. According to a popular myth, a soccer-playing schoolboy picked up the ball and started running with it. The idea caught on, and by 1870s the Rugby Football Union came into being. The game was exported to the United States, and evolved into what is known in Britain as American football.

The game, widely played in schools and colleges is fast-paced and often exciting. The season runs from September to April. It is not as generally popular as soccer.

To complicate matters, there are two versions of the game: rugby union, with teams composed of fifteen players and rugby league, with its heartland mainly in the north and teams consisting of thirteen members. In both versions, most points are scored by a touchdown, called a *try*, with additional points available if the try is *converted*. In rugby union games, in particular, a common sight is the *scrum*, when the forwards of both teams push and shove each other for possession of the ball.

Rugby has been successfully exported throughout the British Isles (the Welsh, Scottish and Irish all have strong teams), and in the British Commonwealth. New Zealand and South Africa are among the leading teams.

Tennis

Tennis is a popular summer game in Britain. Municipally and privately-owned courts can be found all over the country. For many, the words "tennis" and "Wimbledon" go together like strawberries and cream. The All England Championships traditionally take place in June. You'll see saturation coverage on television and radio and commentators become household names.

Despite the popularity of the sport in Britain, it's a source of great irritation to the Brits. They haven't produced a female Wimbeldon champion since Virginia Wade in 1977 or a male champion since Fred Perry, way back in 1935. The damp, gray climate and poor funding for the sport is inevitably blamed.

Golf

Britain is proud possessor of some of the finest golf courses in the world - not surprising - the game was born here. Maybe this explains why, despite its size, Britain produces some of the world's finest golfers. This is one of the sports where Britain does hold its own. The unpredictable weather can actually help.

The Royal and Ancient Golf Club, at St. Andrew's near Edinburgh, is often referred to as "the home of golf." Its roots go back as far as the fifteenth century. The *Old Course* is the focus of most visitors' attention. No fewer than 24 British Opens have been played here. It's also home to a number of international tournaments.

The course is beautiful. On the coast, its layout is largely molded by Mother Nature. Strong winds off the North Sea make it a challenge even for the most experienced.

Some other famous courses in Britain are those at Troon and Gleneagles, also in Scotland, and Royal Lytham, Sunningdale and Wentworth in England. Municipal and private courses abound.

Hockey

Mention the word "hockey" to a Brit, they'll assume you're talking about the game played on grass. (It is called "field hockey" in North America to distinguish it from the immensely popular ice hockey.) Field hockey is played in schools universities, local and regional leagues and international games. Ice hockey is generally confined to the larger towns and cities.

Polo

Only about five hundred polo players play in Britain. This may be because this is a rich man's sport Known as "the sport of kings," it's no coincidence Britain's heir to the throne, Prince Charles, is an avid player of this game.. For that reason alone, the game gets coverage out of all proportion to its size. Polo was imported into Britain by army officers stationed in India

Croquet

Croquet is a summer outdoor game introduced to Britain from France in the mid 1800s. It's not particularly popular - you need a large, flat lawn to play it. It's another genteel pastime epitomizing everyone's stereotype of the British way of life.

Bowls

Many young Britons participate in the excitement of ten-pin bowling but older folk tend to prefer the outdoor (and sometimes indoor) delights of Bowls. Along with Archery, Bowls has been practiced since ancient times. Requirements are a jack (a small ball no less than 2½ inches in diameter nor more than ten ounces in weight), a few sets of bowls, (they must not exceed 16½ inches in circumference and 34½ pounds in weight.) The most important ingredient is the green - a spiffing lawn 42 yards square, with 6 rinks and a ditch 6 inches wide all round.

Bowling clubs flourish, especially in areas with large retired populations. It's fairly easy to glimpse teams of cream-flanneled pensioners battling it out behind tall privet hedges on a warm summer's day. The game is played at the county and international levels, as well as in local clubs.

Snooker

Much like pool, snooker has its origins in pubs and workmen's clubs. In recent years it has reached new heights of popularity, mainly due to its suitability for the small (especially colour) screen. Millions of people stay up into the small hours of the morning to watch the World Championships. Its leading protagonists are household names.

Horse Racing

As far back as the twelfth century, horse racing has been practiced in Britain. The sport is as popular as it has ever been, both from the point of view of the horse owners (Her Majesty the Queen owns several) and the millions who indulge in the habit of laying bets. You'll find a bewildering choice of bookmakers' (bookies) shops (Ladbroke's and William Hill are two) on virtually every street corner. A substantial proportion of the nation's population *has a flutter* (makes bets) in the Grand National held at Aintree, a 4½ mile track near Liverpool.

Races are televised most afternoons on one or more of the major networks. They are held at locations all over the country, both on the flat and over hurdles (National Hunt racing).

Race tracks are always grass. Sufficient time is allowed between each meet for the grass to recover. Races are frequently postponed due to soggy conditions. The state of the race surface - soft, good, firm - plays a major part in the deliberations of both bookies and betters.

Other famous races include the Derby (pronounced "Darby") held at Epsom near London, and the St. Ledger, at Doncaster in Yorkshire.

Attending the races during Ascot Week is considered a high point in the nation's social season. It has enjoyed royal patronage for over 250 years. In the Royal Enclosure, men wear top hats and women wear their latest designer outfit - often accompanied by an outrageous hat. In case anyone had forgotten - the 2½ mile Ascot Gold Cup is the high-spot of Britain's flat-racing season.

Fishing

Fishing is immensely popular in Britain - to be expected in a nation with a long shoreline, countless harbors, estuaries and islands. However, this favorite British pastime is hardly confined to the sea. Inland, ponds and lakes, streams and rivers provide a teeming variety of freshwater fish. Inland waters are being cleaned up and fish are now spotted in the once badly-polluted lower section of the Thames.

There are three main types of fishing. Sea fishing, or angling, requires no permit. Course fishing includes all fish, except trout or salmon, in freshwater rivers and lakes. Some stretches of water require no license, others require a permit and fee.

Equipment needed includes rod and line, bait

(most often maggots, readily available from fishing tackle shops), a portable stool, and a very large umbrella.

Finally, there's game fishing. Most game fishing in Britain is private and out-of-bounds to outsiders, unless you are on a specialist game-fishing vacation. Some clubs and private associations do issue permits, often at sky-high prices.

Information about fishing is available from fishing tackle shops and often includes advice about local conditions.

Other Sports

Other popular sports in Britain include boxing (though after a spate of recent deaths there have been calls to ban the sport), motor racing (Britain has produced an impressive number of formula 1 champions) and swimming. Basketball and its cousin, netball are played in schools, colleges and local leagues. North American sports, including baseball and football have a small, but devoted following.

Chapter Twenty-Two

HOMES

"An Englishman's home is his castle."
English proverb

Britain is a small country. It has just 93,000 square miles of territory, including Northern Ireland, compared with the United States's 3.5 million square miles and Canada's 3.85 million. Nearly sixty million people live in this small space.

When you also take into account that 90% of the land in Britain is owned by less than 10% of the population, you'll realize living conditions in Britain are considerably more cramped than in the U.S. or Canada.

One of the consequences is people live in smaller homes. The psychological desire to own land one senses in North America doesn't seem to be as apparent. Driving from the airport to your accommodations, you'll notice British homes are built closer together and are more uniform in style.

The distinction between urban and rural areas is very clear in Britain. It is frequently possible to find relatively desolate countryside within fifteen or twenty minutes from a bustling city centre.

The strong feeling that the countryside belongs

to everyone is prevalent. Large tracts of it are accessible for walking, often along public rights of way that have been protected by law for centuries. You will notice a comparative lack of "Trespassers will be prosecuted" and "Posted" signs. Public bodies are set up to monitor this.

Dense forests once covered the whole of Britain but only small pockets remain today. The ancient woodland was destroyed to create agricultural land to feed a fast-growing population and provide the wood that was a major source of building material until Elizabethan times.

Since the Industrial Revolution, homes have generally been built of bricks and mortar. Concrete is also commonly used, especially in the construction of larger blocks of *flats* (apartments).

Until recently, it could hardly be said the British are a nation of homeowners. A high proportion of the population lived in property rented either from a private landlord or from local councils, responsible for their upkeep and maintenance.

After World War II, huge, uniform *council estates* were built to accommodate the vast numbers of returning soldiers and their families. For a low rent, the families received basic accommodations with a small garden.

This trend continued well into the 1960s and 70s. Margaret Thatcher, in a deliberate attempt to create a home owning society, reversed it. Mrs.

Thatcher's government allowed council house (public housing) tenants to purchase - for well below the market price - the properties they occupied. This created, almost overnight, a nation of homeowners. (more apt to vote Conservative). Today, more than 60% of the population own their own homes.

House prices skyrocketed in the 1980s. With high mortgage rates, mortgage applications from first-time buyers slumped. Those who already owned homes found it difficult to keep up with the higher mortgage interest payments. Many lost their homes as a result of foreclosure.

By the mid-1990s, prices had in some cases halved and interest rates were at the lowest they had been for many years. However, *estate agents* (realtors) were still having difficulty in finding buyers and sellers.

Note: In Britain, long-term mortgages are normally repayable over twenty-five years.

More than anything else, a house in Britain is a status symbol. The dream of middle class or aspiring middle class families all over the country is to own a detached house, bungalow or flat in the suburbs - even if it's only an inch away from the neighbors. The name of the suburb is important to them also. An accompanying garage is further evidence one has arrived.

The next best thing is to own a *semi-detached house* (a duplex). Vast numbers of these exist in the suburbs of London and all over the country, usually in tree-lined, grass-verged streets. Sir John Betjeman, former Poet Laureate, named the seemingly endless sprawl of semi-detached homes in the west and north London suburbs "Metroland" after the Metropolitan Tube line which services the vicinity. Most British cities have their own metrolands.

A person might have to settle for a *terraced house* (row house), a *flat* (apartment), rent from a private landlord or from the local council (provided you've lived locally for a specified period of time) if you can't aspire to own a detached or semi-detached house.

Depending on your wealth and requirements, a house, bungalow or flat usually comprises a living room (sometimes called the lounge or front room), a small dining room, a kitchen, a bathroom (literally a room with a bath which may or may not contain a toilet), one or two toilets and two or three bedrooms.

Whatever kind of home a Brit has, you're bound to find certain features.

The vast majority of homes in Britain are supplied with clean, drinkable water by a local water authority (once nationalized, recently privatized under John Major). It is usually not necessary to install filters or such. Generally speaking, only rural dwellings have their own wells. Consequently, tap water is nearly always drinkable. If you prefer, bottled water is available at most supermarkets. Don't be surprised if your British host is upset when you insist on using bottled water.

The electrical supply in Britain comes from the *National Grid*. At 240 volts, it's almost enough to melt the innards of your luxury hair drier or incinerate your electric curlers. Electrical sockets are shaped differently from their American and Canadian counterparts. Three rectangular holes in the wall are usually accompanied by an on/off switch.

Until recently, one of the most irritating aspects of buying anything electrical in Britain is you nearly always needed to purchase the plugs separately, making sure the fuse ampage matches that of the appliance. Then there was the fiddly job of fitting the plug to the appliance which required the use of a small screwdriver and all the dexterity of a brain surgeon. Thankfully, most appliances now come with fitted plugs.

The telephone system in Britain has improved considerably over the past ten years. British Telecom, previously a government-owned monopoly, was privatized in the 1980s. It's by far the nation's largest telephone company but telephone services are also provided by other companies. Most of the old fashioned phone sockets have been replaced by phone jacks. In most British homes you'll find at least two of them, usually one in the hallway and one in the master bedroom. A variety of services are operated by the telephone company, and are listed in the telephone directory.

Many touchtone phones are in service these days, but there are still rotaries about. To make most local calls, just dial the number with no prefix. If you can't get through, it may mean you need to use a local prefix of up to three digits. Check the front of the directory.

Long distance calls within the country require prefixing the number with a local code. The code is usually included as part of the number.

To make international calls, dial 001 then the number in North America (it's actually easier than dialing a number in the UK).

Reach the operator by dialing 100.

For directory enquiries (directory assistance) call 192 wherever you are.

Being "unlisted" in Britain is called being *ex-directory.*

Calling 999 anywhere in the country will connect you with emergency services.

British central heating systems have long been a source of wonder and amazement to North American travelers. A family from Massachusetts, spending the winter in Oxford commented on the abundance of external plumbing on the house they were renting. They feared the pipes might freeze.

"Don't worry about the pipes *outside* freezing," advised friends back home, "it's the pipes *inside* you have to worry about." Literature provided to American families relocating to Britain advises them rooms are generally at least 15° cooler.

There's a basic difference in ethos. In America and Canada, due to the greater extremes of winter and the chance your pipes might freeze, heating is kept on all day and night if only at a minimal temperature. The heat is boosted at the thermostat when required.

Where it exists in Britain, central heating is there to make you feel warm and comfortable when you get up and when you get home from work. A time switch located close to the boiler (usually found in the kitchen) ensures the oil or gas-fired radiators and the water heating system come on at least twice a day.

You'll heat whatever small area you're occupying with an electric portable heater (fan or radiant) or a gas heater if you're at home during the day. Every time you go to the bathroom, especially to take a bath or shower, you'll get *goose pimples* (goose bumps).

Other common forms of heating include night storage heaters. They store electricity at night at lower rates and release the heat the following day. Of course, there are real fires fueled by logs or by coal.

The main motivation behind the Brits' reluctant use of central heating is that heating oil and/or gas are much more expensive than in America.

British homes are far more energy-efficient these days than they have been in the past, thanks mainly to *double glazed* (double-layered) windows that keep drafts out and heat in and better insulation of homes.

Americans staying in Britain during the summer are astounded by the lack of door and window screens. Even more horrifying, Brits are apt to keep their screenless windows open day and night. To start with, Britain doesn't have the same horrendous problem with pesky mosquitos continental North America does. The occasional gnat, house fly, wasp or daddy longlegs flying around doesn't bother the intrepid Brit.

Nor will you find storm windows and doors. Britain certainly gets its fair share of savage storms but rarely, if ever, of the ferocity of Bob or Caroline, Ted or Alice.

Cooling systems are rarely to be found in homes, except those belonging to the extremely wealthy. They're simply not needed the majority of the time. Occasionally an exceptionally hot summer, such as that of 1995, comes along and everyone wishes they had air conditioning. Then they console themselves with the knowledge they won't need to use it again for ten years.

Most British homes are linked to a town sewage system. Most homes with septic tanks or cesspools are found in rural areas.

You'll probably wonder what that strange humming sound is outside if you're staying in a British home and find yourself wide-awake at 4 AM. It's probably the milkman on his milk *float* - an almost silent electric vehicle loaded with *pints* and other dairy products.

Later on, the *postman* (mailman) arrives on the first of two deliveries. He or she delivers mail directly into your home through the *letter box* (watch out if you have a dog who likes tasty letters, but never mind the bills). Then comes the paper boy or girl. Depending on the day of the week, you may get a visit from the gas or electricity company.

At least you won't get certain department stores phoning at dinnertime to sell you vinyl siding.

A Typical British Home:

Exterior

Your semi-detached house is like a Siamese twin, except the other twin is painted a different colour. A waist-high brick wall divides the house from the pavement and from the twin.

The twenty foot deep front garden is laid to lawn with the exception of a ten by six flower bed containing roses. The garden is inhabited by concrete painted gnomes, one of which sports a fishing rod - though the small goldfish pond was filled in years ago.

An area is set aside for parking the family car

(there's no garage since the house was built in the 1920's before cars became popular).

Semi-circular windows on both floors allow light to filter in. The houses' red brick walls on the ground floor give way to a covering of pebble dash on the upstairs (first) floor and there is an additional, small window. The house has a gray slate roof and a chimney.

A paved, flower-bordered path leads from the gate to the front door. It is a step above the ground with a tiny porch protecting a visitor from the elements. The door is glazed.

A House Tour

You enter by the frosted glass front door which immediately gives you status (tradesmen must go to the back door). You then enter the hallway. A hat and coat stand invites you to remove your outer layers of garments. Straight ahead a carpeted staircase leads to the bedrooms.

However, you turn left into the living room, or *lounge*, where your nose is first to sense a battle for aerial superiority between cans of furniture polish and several bowls of strategically-placed potpourri. A bay window affords a delightful view of the house opposite. The net curtains ensure that the neighbors can't see inside your home. This British version of Bay Watch conjures up quite a different image from its Californian namesake.

Finally, the room is dominated by a television set, complete with a video (VCR) which faces away from the window so the neighbors can't see what you're watching.

A fireplace is set against the far wall. Its mantelpiece is occupied by a medley of ornaments, including a battery-operated glass clock and various souvenirs from Benidorm. In the fireplace itself, an electric fake coal fire imitates the burning of real coal by means of a stroboscopic flickering of its orange-red bulb. A tiger rug warms itself snugly in front of the fire.

Various prints hang from picture hooks and a lampshade dangles from a central point in the yellowing ceiling.

You make your way to the kitchen, passing the most important closet in the house. It is located under the stairs and all manner of goodies are stored there.

By American standards, British kitchens are small and inadequately equipped. Of course, it has a *cooker* (stove). It might be gas or electric and will have an eye-level grill and oven. A washing machine may be in the kitchen but not always a dryer - there's bound to be a washing line out in the garden. The fridge with a small freezer compartment about the size of your microwave back home is the sole source of ice cubes (Brits rarely put more than one ice cube in their drinks). The microwave, about the size of your toaster back home and assorted electrical appliances such as an iron, toaster, coffee maker are in the kitchen. By far the most important device of all is an electric kettle. These ingenious devices boil water in a very few minutes, usually switching themselves off automatically. Purely delightful for the at-least-ten-cups-of-tea-a-day British.

A kitchen sink with separate hot and cold taps (no mixer or spray) is close by. There are various worktops, cupboards and drawers and possibly a table and chairs if the room is big enough. Somewhere, in a cupboard, there's a rusty charcoal barbecue unused for years because it hasn't been warm enough outside.

A frosted-glass door invites you across the kitchen's linoleum floor to the back garden, via a sunroom with exotic semi-tropical plants and the family freezer.

After two cups of tea, you want to go to the bathroom.

"Oh, you mean the loo," your host responds. He takes great delight in offering a choice of loos to visit. "There's one opposite the top of the stairs - or you can go downstairs if you like." This family really has arrived. In Britain, many upstairs bathrooms contain loos, while the downstairs w.c. (water closet) is little more than precisely that - a closet with a washbasin. Britons never talk about having 1½ bathrooms.

British toilets are referred to with a variety of alternatives to the word "loo," such as *lav, barsy, bog*. They all flush in a charmingly different way from their American counterparts. A level on the cistern, or in older homes a chain, releases a cascade of water, the very force of which is able to do the job (no swirling clockwise movement - just that powerful cascade).

Heating the loo is not one of life's great priorities, so be prepared for a cold seat. *Extractor fans*(vent fans) are not always present, either.

You head upstairs, holding on to the attractive gloss magnolia-painted bannister. First, check the bathroom. It will always contain a bathtub and a washbasin, possibly a toilet. Built-in showers are increasingly common. What you'll often find is a temporary rubber concoction affixed to the bathtub faucets with a flimsy curtain to hide your gorgeous body from any onlooker.

Both bathtub and washbasin may have separate hot and cold taps with no mixer. Hot water may be provided straight from the boiler or from a special water heater (immersion or Ascot) It may either be in the bathroom itself or lurking close by. You'll soon know because of the earth-shattering noise it makes. Be prepared to freeze to death in the bathroom, especially in the dead of winter.

You are now outside the bathroom on the landing. You decide to explore the 12' x 12' master bedroom. Its bay window offers the same, panoramic view of the neighbor's house as the downstairs lounge, except a bit more spectacular - you can see just beyond the gas works.

The focal point of this carpeted, wallpapered room is a double bed covered with a very thick *duvet* (comforter). This is suitable, since the only heating is provided by a night storage heater under the window. In Britain, there are only double and single beds. The terminology "queen" and "king" beds means nothing at all to Brits.

Notice the absence of an *en suite* bathroom and even an *en suite* closet. All the hangable clothes are kept in a wardrobe that doesn't quite seem wide enough.

A dressing table is stationed in the window bay blocking most of the light coming in. Another chest of drawers stands sentinel against the inside wall. On the wall opposite, a fireplace has been filled in.

Lighting is provided via a central lampshade and by two lamps adorning their respective bedside tables.

As Herbert Beerbohm Tree once said, "The national sport of England is obstacle racing. People fill their rooms with useless and cumbersome furniture and spend the rest of their lives trying to dodge it."

The two other bedrooms are much smaller - too small to swing a kitten. They both have nice views - not only of your own back garden, but next door's as well.

With the tour of the house complete, there

remains only the garden. Return downstairs, head out the back door and through the sunroom. The garden is tiny by most American standards - only a little wider than the house and about 50 feet long, enclosed by six feet high wooden fences. It is amazing what it has been made into. A small paved area enclosed by lovingly tended flowering geraniums and lobelias leads on to a lawn. Around it flower beds host a dazzling assortment of plants.

Further on, a low privet hedge divides the space again. A grass path leads through an area thick with growing vegetables - prize-winning marrows and runner beans - to a work shed and a greenhouse. Tomatoes ripen far more quickly in it than their colleagues outside do. It's easy to see why the British spend hours in their gardens.

P.S. Fido, the British dog, lives indoors.

SECTION FOUR

OUTDOOR LIFE

Chapter Twenty-Three

THE COUNTRYSIDE

"To sit in the shade on a fine day and look upon verdure is the most perfect refreshment."
Jane Austen: Mansfield Park (1814)

Few nations can match Britain for the beauty of its countryside, shaped by the interaction of people with nature over many thousands of years. This interaction has produced a fascinating cultural heritage of landscapes, buildings and other artifacts sure to delight everyone who is able to get away from the urban centres to experience it.

Only relatively small fragments of the vast ancient forests that once covered Britain now remain and they are mostly in Wales and Scotland. Much of the woodland was cleared for farming, still more for building material.

The Saxons first implemented the rotational field-system. largely intact to this day. It has given much of the British open space its unique character.

Today, the British countryside is an incredible mixture of landscapes with more shades of green than you ever knew existed. A detailed patchwork quilt is formed by the play of light and shade over fields of crops. The setting of an ancient church or castle; natural landscapes formed by volcanic activity and smoothed down by glaciers; ancient forests of pines, oaks and beeches; purple moorlands, wavebeaten cliffs and windswept marshes - all can be found here.

Even the British weather, changeable as it is, can be an ally. Imagine a wild, wet and windy day watching the Atlantic waves crashing against ancient promontories in Cornwall or Devon or one of the western Scottish islands.

Each corner of Britain has a beauty all its own. Picture yourself on a still summer's afternoon perched high on a hill above the winding River Wye on the England-Wales border or sitting in a lush Dorset garden enjoying a clotted cream tea. Even in winter you will be emotionally moved on a snowy winter's morning in the shadow of Cairngorm.

The British love the countryside and have taken considerable steps to protect it. Conscious of the ugly urban sprawl blighting many landscapes, they have set up green belts around London and other large urban centres to safeguard the countryside from urban encroachment with some success. However, not quite enough to prevent the mushrooming of out-of-town shopping malls and housing developments - especially in the past ten years

In Britain, you're very conscious of leaving the town behind as soon as you get past the city limits. The density of urban development is quickly superseded by open fields, moors, or dense forest. The countryside is interspersed only occasionally by an isolated cottage or farm or by a small hamlet, complete with ancient church and cottages.

Much of Britain's countryside - outside the areas designated for conservation or recreation - is used for agriculture. You will find dairying in the south and west and sheep and cattle rearing in the hilly and moorland regions in the south and west. Arable farming, pig and poultry farming and horticulture are concentrated in the south and east. Nearly 12 million hectares are under crops and grass.

By the early 1990s, the agriculture industry employed 2.1% of the British workforce, and Britain was self-sufficient in about 58% of all types of food and animal feed.

The best way of exploring the countryside in depth is to walk, ride a horse or cycle. Britons are avid walkers. The countryside is dotted with public rights of way whose integrity is jealously protected by the myriad of hikers' and ramblers' organizations. A developer who recently built a house across a public right of way was ordered to demolish the home, or to allow ramblers to walk through the house!

Much of Britain's long shoreline is accessible too. Whole stretches of coast, hundreds of miles long are designated as coastal paths. Public transportation, though depleted in rural areas, still enables travelers to reach destinations fairly quickly and once there, explore on foot or bike.

As a general rule, when crossing agricultural

land keep to the marked paths, the official rights of way marked on Ordnance Survey maps. Otherwise, unless signs indicate, barbed wire fences or landmines (only joking) are in place or it is obvious in some other way that you are not welcome. The land is widely accessible - at your own risk.

For most late twentieth century visitors with only a limited time to see as much as possible, undoubtedly the best way to explore the British countryside is by car. Get off the motorways (M roads), trunk roads (A) and other highways which expedite long-distance travel and travel on the B roads and other unclassified roads and lanes - generally more scenic and slower.

Britain's network of country backroads is exceptional in its own right. The narrow, winding lanes may have started life as a cow path or perhaps a pedestrian short-cut long before the wheel was invented, let alone the motor car!

Lanes are hemmed in on both sides by tall hedgerows separating the fields. They provide an eco system of their own and are a unique part of the national heritage - living, flowering partitions in a rotational field-system centuries old. Though for many farmers they are an irritant, getting in the way of more efficient (and therefore more profitable) farming, their future survival has been ensured by law.

Large tracts of the countryside are protected in a network of National Parks and Forests, while dozens of buildings of historical or architectural interest have been purchased by the National Trust to be preserved for posterity. Others are safeguarded by government-sponsored English Heritage. For example, historic Scotland and Cadw, Welsh historic monuments.

English Nature, the Countryside Council for Wales and Scottish Natural Heritage are responsible for nature conservation in their areas. This includes the management of nature reserves, identifying sites of special scientific interest, supporting and conducting research. These organizations care for some of Britain's most entrancing scenery and stunning stately homes and castles.

National Trust

The National Trust is a registered charity totally independent of government control. It was established in 1895 to forever protect and maintain various national assets, natural and man-made. The Trust maintains the unique statutory power to declare land inalienable. That is, it cannot be sold, mortgaged or compulsorily-purchased against the Trust's wishes without special parliamentary procedures.

In a nation so conscious of its historical and geographical heritage, perhaps it's not surprising that the Trust has heaped up such a wealth of goodies over the past century: Today the organization owns over nearly 600,000 acres of countryside, forests, woods, fens, farmland, downs, moorland and archaeological remains and over 550 miles of coastline.

Included in this veritable treasury are over 200 of England and Wales' historic homes, gardens and 25 monuments. It owns famous sites like Stonehenge, St. Michael's Mount, part of Hadrian's Wall and lesser known places such as Thomas Hardy's cottage at Lower Bockhampton, Dorset; glorious Stourhead Gardens, Wiltshire; and George Washington's ancestral home, Tyne and Wear. Practically all of them are open to the public.

A further 100 properties in Scotland are maintained by the affiliated National Trust for Scotland.

Much of the land and buildings owned by the Trust has come into its possession as the result of donations and bequests. Its annual income of more than £142 million is mostly raised through membership subscriptions, admission charges (unless you're a member), gifts and legacies. In addition, over 30,000 people donated 1.7 million hours of unpaid time to the Trust - worth £5 million (1995).

Virtually all the Trust's income is spent on the care and maintenance of the land and buildings in its protection. Despite this, four out of five of its historic buildings operate at a loss.

In 1995, its centenary year, over 11 million people visited the properties where the number of visitors is recorded. It's estimated four or five times this number visited other areas owned by the Trust where such records are not kept, such as at its many stretches of open countryside.

Nearly every American visitor is likely to encounter at least two or three National Trust or National Trust for Scotland properties when on vacation in the U.K.

The *National Trust Handbook* is a comprehensive guide to the properties. It is available from most bookstores in the U.K., from the National Trust stores throughout Britain and from the National Trust, P.O. Box 39, Bromley, Kent, BR1 3XL, England.

Another resource is the Royal Oak Foundation, the Trust's U.S. not-for-profit membership affiliate, supported by more than 30,000 Americans. Its membership package includes the *Handbook*, free admission to most Trust properties and other materials. Its address is: 285 West Broadway, New York, NY 10013. Telephone: (212) 966-6565. Fax: (212) 966-6619.

The Seasons

Britain's countryside looks great at any time of the year, but spring and summer are particularly attractive. First signs of burgeoning new life appear in March. By April cascades of daffodils bedeck the hedgerows and verges and the birds are in full throttle.

By early summer, the countryside is a thousand shades of green. In late August, golden fields of corn (in Britain, "corn" is a general term given to several arable crops, especially wheat) wave in the cooler breeze much the same way they did during Saxon times.

Fall is pretty, especially in the New Forest or the Scottish Highlands, but don't expect the spectacular vividness of foliage you find in New England.

Bare trees and fields have a melancholy beauty all their own in the winter season. Snow is most likely to fall in the north and east of Scotland, otherwise it is fairly rare. Ponds and rivers rarely, if ever, freeze over.

Farm Animals

Britain's livestock includes around 11 million cattle, 7½ million pigs and 29 million sheep. Poultry includes chickens, turkeys, pheasants. The last of these need to be avoided while driving in country lanes.

Crops

Britain's generally-rich soil combined with highly-efficient farming methods yields a veritable harvest of crops. However, its not enough to feed the sixty million people who live here, let alone the tourists.

Main crops are wheat, oats, barley and rye. Sugar beet and potatoes, an integral part of the British diet is grown in the east of England. *Maize*, known to Americans as corn, is increasingly grown in the south of England.

Visitors to Britain in late spring may wonder what is growing in the dazzling yellow fields. It is rape seed, which produces a fine oil for cooking.

Marrows, broccoli, cabbage, turnips, onions, carrots, peas, cucumbers, tomatoes, beans and cauliflowers are all produced domestically. Squash is something of a novelty, although its relative, the zucchini (known in Britain by its French name, *courgette*) does well.

South of London, the county of Kent is known as the Garden of England, mainly because of all the fruit it produces - primarily apples, pears and plums. The climate is not suitable for more exotic fruits like oranges, lemons or bananas, but grapevines will grow, almost entirely in southern England. There is a small wine industry.

The Country Code

1. Where possible, try to keep to established paths and tracks. If you have to cross a field, avoid going straight across. If you stay close to the fence, you can be sure of not doing any damage to growing crops and are less likely to have damage done to you by an irate farmer.

281

2. Leave all gates as you find them. A closed gate should be closed behind you, an open one left open. When climbing over a gate, do so at the hinge end - it puts less strain on the hinges.
3. Take care not to damage fences and hedges when getting over them.
4. Be careful of livestock. If there is a bull in the field, don't go into that field. Never go near a flock of sheep, especially if you have a dog with you. Sheep are easily alarmed and will run away if frightened. In the lambing season (from December to April) a frightened ewe may lose her unborn lamb.
5. If you are told you are trespassing, apologize and leave immediately.
6. Never leave litter. Waste paper, banana skins, cans and other garbage should be collected and disposed of in a proper place. Quite apart from the unsightly appearance of garbage scattered through the countryside, sharp cans and broken glass may harm livestock and other people, and glass may also start a fire.
7. Never camp or light a fire on private ground without asking permission. Always make sure that the fire is properly out when you leave.
8. Never light a fire on grass or in woodland. Choose a bare patch of earth, and, if possible, confine the fire within a circle of stones or rocks.

9.   Never eat berries unless you know what they are. There are many poisonous berries in the British countryside.
10.   It is tempting to pick wild flowers but try not to do so unless you are taking them straight home. Some flowers, like bluebells, die very quickly, even if put in water at once. Many plants and flowers are protected by law, and digging them up could result in a hefty fine.

Wildlife

Britain's abundant wildlife includes some unique species. Insectivores include the hedgehog, a shy creature commonly found in city parks and gardens, as well as the countryside; the mole, found everywhere; and four varieties of shrew.

Thirteen varieties of bats thrive. They include the pipistrelle, the smallest of British bats. It lives in rock crevices, trees and buildings. Another is the rare mouse-eared bat. It never ventures away from its habitat in caves and buildings in Dorset.

Rabbits, introduced into Britain by the Normans, are widespread in woods and grassland. They have recovered from the outbreaks of myxomatosis in the 1950s. The brown hare is found mainly in open country on chalk and limestone below 2,000 feet. The Mountain hare, as its name suggests, thrives on the open moors and rocky slopes of the Scottish Highlands and Ireland.

Rodents found in Britain include the red squirrel. It was once common, but since the introduction of the gray squirrel to Britain between 1876 and 1929, its numbers have reduced dramatically. It is found in some conifer forests, mostly in Scotland, with a few surviving pockets in England, including Brownsea Island, Dorset.

Britain's mice population include the Harvest Mouse, found in buildings, corn ricks and hedgerows; the Wood Mouse and Yellow-necked Mouse, both found in hedgerows and woods everywhere and the House Mouse, the small variety found in Britain.

The Edible Dormouse was introduced into Britain in only 1902 and is found mainly in deciduous woods and lofts of buildings. As its name suggests, it was once regarded as a delicacy. The Dormouse thrives in woodland, especially where there are beech or hazel trees.

Varieties of vole include the Bank Vole, found in deciduous woods, scrub and hedgerows; the Orkney Vole, found in pastures and arable land everywhere; the Short-tailed Vole which just adores rough grassland; and the Water Vole - commonly known as the Water Rat - found on the banks of lowland canals, ponds, slow running rivers and streams.

The Coypu was introduced about 1930. It became wild after escaping from fur farms. It is most likely to be found in the river banks, reed beds and marshes of East Anglia.

The Black Rat was very common in Britain in the Middle Ages. It is suspected to be the vector that brought the Black Death (Bubonic Plague) to the country. It has been rare since 1700, except around ports, where it may arrive on ships. The Brown rat is not really a native. It came to Britain in the eighteenth century. It enjoys sharing your home, garbage and waste disposal plants, corn ricks and sewers.

Carnivores (flesh-eating mammals) in Britain include the Pine Marten, very rare these days. The American Mink escaped from fur farms and now breeds in the wild near rivers, streams and lakes, particularly in the south-west. Then there is the Polecat, found in thickets and woods in Wales and the Wild Cat, confined to woods and moorlands in the Scottish Highlands.

The Red Fox has encroached on most urban areas, where it is a fairly common sight. Stoats and weasels are common and can be found in virtually any kind of terrain. The Badger enjoys woods and copses near pasture land in many parts of the country. Otters, very rare in south and south east England, are mainly found in the streams, lakes and marshes along western coasts.

Seals are no strangers to British shores. The Common Seal enjoys sheltered water, including mud and sandbanks and river estuaries. The Grey (Atlantic) Seal prefers the stormier waters off islands and rocky shores with access to the open sea.

The largest native deer in Britain is the Red Deer, indigenous to the Lake District, the Brendon and Quantock Hills, the Scottish Highlands and Isles and Exmoor, Devon. In the summer it moves from the forest to moorland. The Roe Deer is found in open woodland and on the edge of forests, mainly in the south east of England, the Border counties between England and Scotland, and the Lake District.

Fallow Deer can be spotted in the New Forest and Rockingham Forest. Japanese Sika Deer, introduced into parks in the mid-18th century, prefer deciduous or mixed woods with hazel and bracken cover. Other deer escaped from private estates and have survived. These include the Indian and Chinese Muntjac (Barking Deer) and the Chinese Deer. Reindeer once prospered in Britain but by the thirteenth century had become extinct. In recent years, reindeer from Swedish Lapland have been introduced into the Cairngorm region of Scotland.

Other wild animals include the Wild Goat, at home on mountain crags and virtually inaccessible mountain ledges in Scotland, northern England and Wales. Wild Soay Sheep are confined to the island of St. Kilda. White cattle, from Chillingham Park, Northumbria, are descendants of wild forest cattle domesticated in the thirteenth century. Wild Ponies are not strictly wild. They are regularly herded and branded. Breeds include Shetland, Welsh, Exmoor,

Dartmoor, Fell, Highland, and New Forest. The latter are descendants of the horses that escaped from the Spanish Armada.

Britain's one poisonous snake, the Adder (or Viper) lives on dry sandy heaths, open moor, hillsides and marshlands in East Anglia. It is clearly identifiable by a zig-zag pattern down its back. The Grass Snake lives in hedgerows, open woodland and marshes and, along with the rare Smooth Snake, limited to certain heaths and woods in southern England, is harmless.

Harmless too, are Britain's lizards. The Viviparous lizard is found anywhere below 3,000 feet. The Slow Worm looks like a snake because it has no legs. It is common in heaths and gardens, especially in the south and west. The Sand Lizard is very rare, preferring dry open country, heaths and sand dunes.

Pond life includes various newts. Which of the following bears most resemblance to the American Gingrich variety? The Warty Newt is found in deep ponds on clay or chalk. The Smooth Newt is found in most ponds, except in hills, and the Palmate Newt prefers ponds in hilly terrain.

Toads and frogs include the Common Toad, often hidden beneath stones in shady places and hollows; the Natterjack Toad, found on sandy soil at sea level; the Common Frog, widespread, but preferring to be near a pond; the Edible Frog (just try) and the Marsh frog, found only in the Rye Marshes, Romney and Walland Marshes of south east England.

The abundance of British insect life is too great to list. Most common encounters will be with spiders, none of which are poisonous. Ants tend to be much smaller than their American counterparts. Crane flies or "daddy long legs" seem to enter every home in the late fall but are quite harmless. There is a variety of moths and butterflies, some rare. Of course, you will find mosquitoes, gnats and midges, all of which may give you a nasty nip. These are usually found in damp areas, especially near rivers and streams.

Birds

Britain is a bird lover's paradise. Information about bird life in Britain is best obtained from the Royal Society for the Protection of Birds. It owns sanctuaries throughout the country. Its address is:
R.S.P.B.
The Lodge
Sandy
Bedfordshire SG19 2DL
England

Chapter Twenty-Four

GARDENS

*"God Almighty first planted a garden; and,
indeed, it is the purest of pleasures."*

Francis Bacon

Visitors to Britain are entranced by the quality
of town and city parks and even more by the beauty
of the many private gardens. Vast landscaped estates
like Stourhead in Wiltshire, were designed by the
master of English landscape "Capability" Brown in
the early 1740s. Tiny urban-backstreet yards and
patios are transformed into horticultural works of art
by enterprising owners. Even where homes have no
outdoor space, well-tended window boxes provide a
riot of color. For the average Brit, the garden is
regarded as an extra room - an extension of the living
space.

Tourists often comment on how remarkably
green the countryside is, even in the summer. The
main cause of the damp, temperate climate is the
Atlantic Ocean. Its weather systems produce rain and
mild temperatures year round. Long daylight hours in
the summer give plants a chance to get a brief, but
important, opportunity to sunbathe even when the
weather is predominantly cloudy.

289

The Anglo-Saxons were highly competent farmers. They first established a rotational field-system for crops that survives to this day.

In early medieval times, wealthy, land owning town and village dwellers set apart sections where they could grow herbs and fruit trees, often within walled enclosures. Monastic communities became almost self-sufficient by growing fruit and vegetables on their land. The famous Covent Garden area of London derives from "Convent Garden." It was once the site of an orchard belonging to Westminster Abbey.

The merit of gardens for leisure purposes was recognized by Elizabethan times. The creation of intricate geometric patterns by the interplay of flower beds and low hedges brought visual delight to many an Elizabethan eye. Further sensual stimulation was provided by the widespread planting of aromatic herbs and vegetables.

The Renaissance period saw the further development of gardening as an art form. Fountains, ponds and statuary were introduced. Landscape gardening became a specialty of the British, led by Lancelot "Capability" Brown in the mid 1700s. The gardens he created at Stourhead, Wiltshire, built round an artificial lake and studded with mock-classical temples and grottos is perhaps his finest work. Stourhead is worth seeing at any time of the year but in spring time, when the azaleas and rhododendrons are in bloom, the effect is stunning. Middle class landowners, realizing the many benefits of well-maintained gardens, began to employ their own gardeners and an industry was born.

The Industrial Revolution brought about an exodus of population from the country to the cities. Cramped, unhealthy housing conditions existed in Jerry-built or *two-up, two-down* terraced homes built quickly and cheaply to accommodate the masses.

These often had only a tiny outdoor space, usually paved and perhaps no more than twenty feet square, surrounded by high brick walls. This was known as the yard. For Brits, the word "yard" still has this connotation, unlike the American yard, often a much larger space.

People interested in growing plants but without enough space adjacent to their home might rent an *allotment* on the edge of town where they could grow vegetables to feed the family.

The merits of gardening as therapy for a variety of physical and mental conditions, as well as its practical benefits as a potential source of food, was recognized. Some of the vast Victorian piles which passed off as mental hospitals included a large, outdoor area where patients could grow plants.

As the housing stock improved between World Wars I and II, the importance of having one's own outdoor space, however small, was stressed. Many new suburbs were built in parklike settings, with grass verges gracing tree-lined streets.

Even in the poorer neighborhoods, new homes inevitably imitated wealthier suburban homes with a small front garden for ornamental purposes, and a larger back garden for leisure use. People could grow vegetables and herbs and use it as a place of escape. Their own little piece of the countryside in town.

During the Second World War there were practical benefits, too. Special radio broadcasts encouraged anyone who had even the smallest plot of land to "dig for victory." Many families built greenhouses to allow for better seed-sowing and the ability to grow certain plants, such as tomatoes, earlier (or later) in the season.

The *garden shed* provided a space for doing messy tasks that could not be performed indoors.

With the coming of the car, many homeowners built garages, which further eroded the amount of space for growing.

Today, the amateur botanist Brits regard their gardens as part of their home. For that reason, however large or small, the back garden is often sheltered and protected from unwelcome prying eyes by high fences, walls or hedges.

The front garden is the showpiece area, frequently a riot of floral colour. These days it is often covered over with pea stone or paving. It may feature a small pond and small, tacky figurines known as garden gnomes - a source of humour and derision.

The back garden serves a variety of purposes. It may be sub-divided into a small paved patio area, then a further area laid to lawn and surrounded by beds containing perennials and smaller flowers. Beyond this, perhaps separated by a hedge or trellis, a plot used to grow vegetables and a greenhouse in the corner can be found.

Brits spend hours tending to their gardens - removing weeds, pruning the roses, clipping the privet hedges and, of course, watering the plants. Mulch has never really caught on, partly because of the absence of extreme frost and partly because they've never thought of it.

Gardening is part of the social round, too. Up and down the country in both rural and urban areas, vegetable and flower growing competitions are held. The privilege of growing the largest marrow (a kind of large zucchini) is a cause of particular pride and envy. Grown men, convinced of the invincibility of their carefully-nurtured marrow, have been reduced to tears by being pipped at the post by a rival marrow. In some ways, the tending is more important than sitting (or lying) down to enjoy the peace and tranquillity of the garden. It certainly is therapeutic.

For the professional botanist, one has to go no further than Kew Gardens, London or the Royal Botanical Gardens in Edinburgh to see rare trees and plants. Some of them are housed in vast greenhouses - earning the name "crystal palaces."

Seaside resorts attract visitors as much for their pleasure gardens as for their beaches. It's no coincidence that the resort of Bournemouth uses the slogan "Garden City by the Sea" to attract domestic holiday makers. In 1995, it won the title of being *Europe's Floral City* - a highly prestigious accolade.

When visiting a British home, (unless it's a high-rise apartment) ask to see the garden. It may not be large but your hosts will burst with pride as they show you around.

Gardening is one of Britain's leading leisure activities. As more and more of the countryside disappears under bricks, mortar and concrete, gardens and the art of gardening help to keep Brits healthy in mind, body and soil.

Chapter Twenty-Five

AT THE SEASIDE

"Oh I do like to be beside the seaside."
Popular music hall song by John A.Glover-Kind

The old music-hall song says it all - Brits are obsessed with the sea. That's not surprising in a country where no one lives more than 100 miles from the coast. In fact, no one in Britain *can* live more than 100 miles from the coast.

Perhaps this fascination with the sea has something to do with the fact Britain's separation from the rest of Europe by water has protected it from the kind of invasions that frequently plagued other continental nations. The English Channel is known as England's Moat for good reason.

Maybe it is related to history. Britain, until the early part of this century boasted the largest navy in the world and the largest merchant fleet.

Or, it could be because much of Britain's sustenance has come from fish and other sea creatures. British blood, it seems, is a good deal saltier than most.

Most Brits relish a visit to the seaside, whether for a day trip on a wet Bank Holiday, or for their main vacation.

In the late 1700s, a certain Dr. Russell of Lewes, Sussex suggested a visit to the seaside might actually do a person's health a power of good. Ridiculed at first, Russell persisted with the idea. He ventured to suggest taking a dip might be to people's advantage. This novel idea was slow to catch on.

In 1783, the Prince Regent latched on to the idea. He built an exotic royal pavilion, transforming the sleepy fishing village of Brighthelmstone into the fashionable seaside resort of Brighton.

Royal patronage served as a catalyst to attract the wealthy at first. In the mid 1800s the development of the railway system made the seaside accessible to the masses. Other equally sleepy fishing villages were transformed into brash, fun-loving, good-time resorts, and subsequently, retirement havens.

Today it is every Britons' goal in life to uproot himself from family, friends and trustworthy neighbors of years standing when he retires and buy a tiny seaside bungalow,- preferably on the south coast. Long lengths of Britain's southern coastline are choc-a-bloc with residential developments. Certain sections are sometimes referred to as the "Costa Geriatrica."

Many of Britain's seaside resorts are struggling from a crisis provoked largely by the upsurge in inexpensive, all-inclusive vacations to mainland Europe, particularly France, Spain and Greece. The reluctance of Britain's elderly population to contemplate any major change which would enable the resorts to compete with their continental counterparts doesn't help.

When Noel Coward wrote, "Mad dogs and Englishmen go out in the midday sun," he was deadly serious. The Brits are every bit as crazy about the sun as they are about the sea. The combination of sun, with a pinch of sand thrown in for good measure, drives them wild.

British resorts advertise their merchandise liberally - sun, sun and more sun. A slight problem is that the sun really doesn't shine as much as it does on the Costa del Sol or the French Riviera. British stores do a much better trade in umbrellas and raincoats than they do in sun protection factor 15. At least in Britain the beaches are free.

British resorts try to make up for the lack of sunshine in other ways. For example, by flaunting their parks and gardens. Bournemouth, a seaside resort of 150,000 on the south coast, beat off competition from the rest of Europe to win the *Entente Florale* competition in 1995.

For the contest, more than 100 civic gardeners planted more than 280,000 bedding plants at expense of the mainly-assenting local taxpayers. A further 2.5 million bedding plants and 3,000 hanging floral baskets in private gardens and commercial premises further enhanced the scene.

Such spending would cause howls of protest in the U.S. The British feel comforted by knowing if it's too cold to take a dip or sit on the beach, one can take a stroll through the pretty gardens or sit in a deck chair listening to a band in the park playing old favorites immortalized by Tommy Dorsey.

Other resorts tempt day-trippers and longer staying holiday makers with traditional attractions like funfairs. Blackpool has its Pleasure Beach and Southend its Kursaal. Eccentricities abound. For example, the Blackpool Tower - a rusty Eiffel-Tower-like structure rising 519 feet above the Lancashire town is open to the public. Model villages (scale models of a town or village) can be found in a wide variety of locations.

The British seaside resorts doing best are those that have managed to diversity their economies and bring their facilities up to international standards. They cleaned up their beaches; opened conference and convention centers; improved their shopping and entertainment facilities and promoted themselves in non-traditional markets such as continental Europe.

Several south coast resorts have been particularly successful in tapping the large language-school market. At any time during the summer, for example, there may be 20,000 young people from all over the world learning English in Bournemouth's language schools. As well as bringing lire, francs, marks and now rubles to the town, they add a distinctly continental flavor. After all, that is what the British public claims to prefer.

Unlike much of the U.S., where the season begins sharply on Memorial Day and beaches are often deserted after Labor Day, the British beach season begins on any sunny day over 60° and any cloudy day over 70°. The season only ends when the last glimpse of bearably-warm sunshine has disappeared.

The Brit will take a brief paddle with trouser legs rolled up if not of an age or a bearing to take a dip in the briny or to build sand castles. Then they will pull up one of the striped deck chairs rented from the local council. Shielded from the bracing wind by a striped *wind-breaker* (also rented from the local council), they may either doze off or read the *Sun*. The more adventurous may choose to take a walk along the *promenade* (boardwalk).

Note: A windbreaker is a canvas wind shield that protects sunbathers from the prevailing winds.

Britain has mile upon mile of gorgeous sandy beaches. Nearly all of them are open to the public and consequently free (you may have to pay to park your car). Lifeguards cover stretches of the beaches in many of the resorts. You won't find them stuck at the top of ladders as they are in the States. They're usually to be found in the beach office.

Do not enter the water if red flags are flying. Even if it looks calm, there may be undertows.

Another feature of many British beaches are the *groynes* (breakwaters) that help retain the sand. Do not venture near these and certainly never climb on to one.

Changing rooms are sometimes provided. More often than not, Brits will prefer to engage in the ancient ritual of trying to put on or remove their swimming costume draped in an old towel in full view of everyone else on the beach. Topless sunbathing for women is permitted in some areas, much to the surprise of many Americans.

Depending on the quality of the beach, (many of Britain's resorts have pebbly beaches) children will be seen happily building sandcastles with a bucket and spade. Others will be seen playing in the water.

Mom and Dad, competing for the number of goose-pimples (goose-bumps) they can muster, recline in their deckchairs patiently waiting for a glimpse of the all-elusive sun.

Some resorts organize beach games for children. Occasionally, Punch and Judy shows can be spotted. The always attract a large gathering of laughing, spellbound children and fascinated adults recalling their own childhood.

Naturally, in an environment with such changeable weather, most resorts' entertainments are by no means confined to the strand. Piers are a feature of many British resorts. They are usually large Victorian eccentricities serving as jetties for passenger boats and doubling up as amusement centres. Americans exploring the local pier will discover an array of ingredients containing the essence of the British seaside. Cafeterias and *take-away* facilities; seafood kiosks offering vinegar-marinated cockles, mussels and whelks; *candy floss* (cotton candy) and ice cream shops. (One of Britain's ice-cream specials is the 99. A vanilla ice cream-filled cone containing a stick of flaky milk chocolate.)

Here, on the pier, you're likely to find children's rides and fairground-style sideshows, including clairvoyants and fortune tellers with their crystal balls and *What the Butler Saw* machines.

The centerpiece is a theatre. For the duration of the summer season you can see a bawdy comedy romp in the "No Sex Please, We're British" mold. They often feature well-known domestic TV stars. When Brits talk about an *end of the pier* show or joke, it usually means something with a heavily sexual innuendo.

Other pastimes include simply watching people fish from the lower deck or dozing off in a deck chair, lulled to sleep by the sound of the swell beating against the pier's uprights beneath. It's about the closest most people will come to an ocean cruise.

Back on dry land, other typical features of British seaside life are the amusement arcades. They are indoor areas with one-arm bandits and other slot machines. The inevitable bingo section will be there, but don't expect your winnings to be any more than a tiny percentage of what you'd get in Atlantic City or Las Vegas.

While Mom's enjoying an afternoon game of bingo, Dad can take the kids to play *crazy golf* (a miniature golf course full of ornamental obstacles). You can wander round the gardens, stopping to listen to a military band perhaps.

By contrast, you may make your way to the various shops and stores. In addition to plastic raincoats and umbrellas, you can buy buckets and spades, a union flag to stick in your sandcastle and seaside postcards with saucy cartoons that look as if they've been modeled on a Benny Hill skit. Buy a stick of *rock (*A foot long, tooth-shattering stick of peppermint with the name of the resort embedded in its core.)

In the evening, visit one of the non-pier summer variety shows or maybe it's one of the nights when the illuminations are lit. Many British resorts have them. Thousands of electric light bulbs (at Bournemouth, real candles) light the main thoroughfares plus hundreds of additional displays in all shapes and sizes.

Chapter Twenty-Six

THE WEATHER

"When two Englishmen meet, their first talk is of the weather."   Dr. Samuel Johnson

"Rain is good for vegetables, and for the animals who eat those vegetables, and for the animals who eat those animals."
Dr. Johnson, quoted by James Boswell in his "Life of Samuel Johnson." (1763)

Dr. Johnson's observation is just as pertinent today as it was when it was written more than two hundred years ago. The English, and indeed all the inhabitants of the British Isles, are obsessed by the weather.

When you've spent some time in Britain, you'll see exactly why talking about the weather so captivates the Brits. It's an endless pageant of blue skies, menacing clouds, blue skies *with* menacing clouds, frost and dew, balmy and heatwave, ice and snow, drizzle, fog, pouring rain and gale-force winds - and it can be quite changeable the next day, too.

Britain's geographical position on the western edge of the European land mass and on the north-eastern side of the Atlantic Ocean is the key to this varied weather pattern. Whatever is happening over these areas inevitably affects the kind of weather Britain is going to "enjoy." Westerly winds off the Atlantic, for example, bring the relative mildness of the ocean atmosphere in winter and keep summer days more temperate.

Visitors to parts of south-western coastal England, Wales and stretches of Scotland's west coast are astonished to find tall, if somewhat anaemic, palm trees growing. They stand amongst the roses, chrysanthemums and rhododendron bushes in the beautifully-manicured parks and gardens, making them resemble a set from *South Pacific*.

Easterly winds off the European land mass cools down and warms up Britain much faster than the ocean winds. They can bring biting cold in winter (though nowhere near as biting as interior U.S. and Canada) and also balmy heatwaves in the not-quite dog days of summer.

Another factor is the geography of the British Isles. The mountains and hills run like a curved spine from Cornwall in the south west, through Wales, northern England and Scotland (roughly in a line from the River Exe to the River Tyne) and trap much of the moisture. As a consequence, the western areas tend to have substantially more rainfall than eastern Britain.

One result of the British climate's Piscean indecisiveness is the predominance in many British homes, hotels and offices of equally indecisive, antiquated heating systems. You won't find air-conditioning systems except in the more modern office complexes, a few upmarket department stores, and the more expensive hotels.

When the heating and cooling systems do work, such is the cost of fuel that the British are very reluctant to keep them on. Consequently, even mild winter days can feel excruciatingly cold indoors and the few really warm days make indoors intolerable.

A Massachusetts family visiting London for the first time related their horrifying experience of watching a West End musical sitting in the "gods." It was one of the hottest, sultriest nights in London for years and they only had the frantic fanning of their playbills to cool them down.

Much of southern Britain comes to a grinding halt after just an inch or two of snow. Twenty-mile traffic jams caused by melting motorways are not unfamiliar when the temperature rises above 80° in the north.

The most striking feature of the British climate is its changeability. A beautiful, warm summer's morning can quickly give way to a windy, wet afternoon (and vice versa) as any Wimbledon fanatic will testify. 1995 was one of the few years when rain did not stop play at all. Rain stops play in a vast number of cricket matches each year but normally there is just enough dry weather to get on with at least part of the game.

It is quite common to see pinstripe-suited Brits

heading to the office on a bright, cloudless morning sporting a briefcase and a *brolley* (umbrella). Don't trust the weather - still less the weather forecast. After all, this is the country where big mac is something you wear, not eat.

Some of the stereotypes concerning the British weather are quite unfair, or at least, out-of-date. Although the prevailing westerly air flow brings a succession of moist weather systems off the Atlantic, it does not rain for every second of every day, even in Manchester (it just seems to). These Atlantic depressions are just as likely to produce drizzle, showers or plain old cloudiness as they are to produce the kind of torrential, endless rains portrayed in so many Hollywood films.

In fact, the North American visitor may be interested to learn that the skies above Boston, New York, New Orleans, Vancouver and even Rome produce more annual rainfall than those over the British capital.

Another frequent criticism levelled against the British weather is it is always foggy. The *peasouper* fog is featured in just about every film made about Jack the Ripper and in French Impressionist paintings of London. It used to be responsible for the demise of hundreds, even thousands of Brits annually, both as a result of the consequential respiratory difficulties and by walking into lampposts. No wonder London was referred to by the nickname "The Smoke."

The Government's Clean Air Act of 1955 enforced the use of smokeless coal throughout London and in many other urban centres. Since then, fogs have become the exception, rather than the rule. At the same time, the average daily sunshine in London has increased nearly 50%!

Getting Away From the Weather

Every winter, millions of Britons predict another miserable, gray summer. Unwilling to spend another two weeks sitting for hours in striped deckchairs rented at great expense, while waiting for a glimpse of that glittering yellow ball, they book package vacations to Spain, Greece or Italy.

Jurassic British seaside resorts, despite their palm trees, are increasingly recognizing the need to produce more indoor attractions and entertainments. They must compete with their Mediterranean rivals as cheap charter flights devour a crumbling domestic market. The hot summer of 1995 gave something of a respite with increased domestic holiday bookings.

"Wouldn't it be great if we had weather like Spain?" complains the average British holiday maker, who also happens to be an avid gardener. Yes, maybe. However, for all its faults, it's the weather, above all, that has molded the British landscape and keeps the countryside and the gardens so lush, green, attractive and productive.

The Weatherman

Only in Britain could TV weathermen and women become national celebrities. To most people, they are also something of a joke. Despite some of the most sophisticated weather forecasting equipment in the world, they frequently seem to get it completely wrong.

Their most famous misforecast was in 1987. A megastorm that came up in the English Channel was not predicted. The storm, with its 100-mile-per-hour winds, ripped apart much of southern England, caused major structural damage, uprooted ancient trees and caused several deaths. One of the major casualties was the Botanical Gardens at Kew, where hundreds of trees were felled. Even the BBC's national breakfast TV program had to be broadcast from a shed.

In the defence of all weathermen, it must be said that British weather is almost impossible to predict, given the unstable influence of the Atlantic. At least it gives everybody something to talk about.

The most important aspect of the British weather for the North American visitor is not the weather itself - but the opportunity to start a hundred conversations with normally reserved Brits. Just don't be too critical!

Seasons

Spring is normally the driest season, though it may not seem so with the April showers. The climate begins to warm up in late April and may have some surprisingly warm days toward the end of the month.

May can be very pleasant indeed, temperatures occasionally reaching 75° (24°C) over much of the country.

Note: TV and newspaper weather forecasts usually give the temperature in Celsius - to the annoyance of Brits who still think in Fahrenheit.

June is usually Britain's brightest month, with average daily sunshine of around eight hours on the south coast and about five hours in the north.

Around the mid-summer period, it may stay light until 10 or 11 PM, depending on your latitude. July and August are the main vacation months. Though rain tends to increase during the period, it is also the warmest time of the year. Temperatures in the upper 70°s and low 80°s (26°- 27°C) are not uncommon. Once in a while it may exceed 90° (32°C). Nights are comfortable - rarely does the temperature exceed 60° (15°C) at night - even in the warmest months.

The sea is a cooling influence and coastal areas

may be noticeably cooler than places just a few miles inland - depending on the wind direction.

The warm weather often continues until September. During the second half of the month, the weather begins to become more unsettled. Nights become noticeably cooler and trees begin to shed their leaves. The fall brings the first frosts.

Snow may fall on the higher ground of northern Britain as early as October. British winters tend to be grey, damp and drizzly. Occasionally, a sparkling clear sunny day, perfect for a long walk along the shore or through the woods or for nestling with a pint of warm beer in front of the log fire in a country pub comes along. The ground may freeze at night throughout the country but rarely are temperatures below freezing during the day. In parts of the south west of England, it is so mild during the winter that grass grows all year round.

Bibliography

Ashley, Maurice. *The People of England: A Short Social and Economic History.* Baton Rouge, LA: Louisiana State University Press, 1982.

Bradford, Sarah. *The Reluctant King: The Life and Reign of George VI, 1895-1952.* New York: St. Martin Press,1990.

Brereton, Peter. *A Touring Guide of English Villages.* London: Peerage Books, 1992.

Brown, Allen. *English Castles.* Chancellor Press: London, 1970.

Edwards, David L. *The Cathedrals of Britain.* Wilton, CT: Morehouse Publishing..

Frasier, Antonia. *The Wives of Henry VIII.* New York: Vintage Books, 1992.

Kenyon, J.P. Editor. *A Dictionary of British History.* Stein & Day, New York: Scarborough House, Brearcliff Manor, 1981.

Lofts, Norah. *Queens of England.* Garden City NewYork: Doubleday & Company, 1970.

McCrum, Cran, MacNeil. *The Story of English.* New York: Penguin Books, 1986.

Muir, Richard. *Riddles in the British Landscape.*500 Fifth Avenue, NY: Thames and Hudson, Inc.,1981.

Scullard, H.H. *Roman Britain: Outpost of the Empire.* London: Jared and Hudson Ltd., 1979

Smith, Lacey Baldwin. *This Realm of England: 1399 to 1688.* Lexington, MS/Toronto/London: D.C Heath and Company, 1976.

Walmsley, Jane. *Brit-think, Ameri-think.* New York: Penguin Books, 1987.

Wechsler, Robert, Editor. *In a Fog: The Humorist's Guide to England.* Highland Park, NJ: Catbird Press.

Reader's Digest Nature Lover's Library
Animals of Britain
Birds of Britain
Butterflies and Other Insects of Britain
Trees and Shrubs of Britain
Water Life of Britain
Wild Flowers of Britain

London and New York: Reader's Digest

Index

313

314

315

316

317

318

319

320

ORDER FORM

Book Title	Amt	Price	Total
Traveling to Europe Like a Pro		$18.95	
No More Hotels in Paris		$15.95	
American Travelers in Britain		$16.95	
Travel Light		$15.95	
Shipping & Handling *1 book $1.50* *Each added book up to 9, add .75* *Orders of 10 or more books will be invoiced separately*	Subtotal S&H Tax (CA) TOTAL		

California residents please pay 7.25% sales tax.

How to Order

1. Send this coupon with your check or money order.
2. Credit card orders call 800-876-1373 or Fax: 805-984-0503

☐ Check ☐ Money Order ☐ Visa ☐ MasterCard ☐ Amex

Card No. __ __ __ __   __ __ __ __   __ __ __ __   __ __ __ __

Exp. Date: __ __ __ __   Signature_____

NEWJOY PRESS, PO Box 3437, Ventura CA 93006-3437

Name_____

Address_____

City, State, Zip_____

Phone_____Fax:_____

Unconditional Guarantee
If you are not satisfied with your purchase for any reason,
simply return it and your money will be refunded.

325

ORDER FORM

Book Title	Amt	Price	Total
Traveling to Europe Like a Pro		$18.95	
No More Hotels in Paris		$15.95	
American Travelers in Britain		$16.95	
Travel Light		$15.95	

Shipping & Handling	
1 book $1.50	Subtotal
	S&H
Each added book up to 9, add .75	Tax (CA)
Orders of 10 or more books will be invoiced separately	TOTAL

California residents please pay 7.25% sales tax.

How to Order
1. Send this coupon with your check or money order.
2. Credit card orders call 800-876-1373 or Fax: 805-984-0503
   ☐ Check ☐ Money Order ☐ Visa ☐ MasterCard ☐ Amex

Card No. __ __ __ __ __ __ __ __ __ __ __ __ __ __ __ __
Exp. Date: __ __ __ __ Signature_____

NEWJOY PRESS, PO Box 3437, Ventura CA 93006-3437

Name_____

Address_____

City, State, Zip_____

Phone_____Fax:_____

Unconditional Guarantee
If you are not satisfied with your purchase for any reason, simply return it and your money will be refunded.